Crime Against Women and Child

An Emerging Social Problem

Crime Against Women and Child

An Emerging Social Problem

Aadesh K. Devgan

CYBER TECH PUBLICATIONS
4264/3, Ansari Road, Daryaganj, New Delhi-110002 (India)
Ph.: 011-23244078. Fax: 011-23280028
E-Mail: cyberpublicationsdelhi@yahoo.com

Crime Against Women and Child—An Emerging Social Problem

First Edition 2008

Reprinted 2025

Published by G.S. Rawat

For Cyber Tech Publications

4264/3, Ansari Road, Daryaganj, New Delhi - 110 002

E-mail : cyberpublicationsdelhi@yahoo.com

Phone : 011-23244078,

Fax : 011-23280028

Printed at

Amit Enterprises, Moujpur, Delhi. Ph. - 9810878184

Preface

This book Crime Against Women and Child is an emerging challenges and other issues are articulated comprehensively. The biological weakness of a women makes her an easy prey particularly to physical domination. She is often a victim of physical violence not only outside her home but also in her home. Added to that the constant neglect of the female children, which apart from having adverse effect on their health also creates mental conditions for them in which they cannot resist any physical violence or several forms of injustices.

Unfortunately, women have been discriminated in all spheres of life in all societies with varied magnitude and dimensions all through the ages. Various types of crimes and atrocities are inflicted on them. Rape, wife beating, eve teasing, sexual and physical harassment, economic exploitation etc. are some of worth crimes, and modern women frequently faces.

The student of marketing must develop a facility for integrating useful contributions from many disciplines.

Last but not the least my publishers who appreciated this book and brought this work out in a record time.

—*Editors*

Contents

CHAPTER 1

Crime Against Women and Child: Social Problem

Every civilized society accepting the importance of equality of sexes has, therefore, made affirmative provisions against gender discrimination. But in spite of enactment of these provisions, equality between men and women continues to be an eluded goal. The reasons for such a wide gap between the ideal and the practical is not only due to historical reasons but mainly because of attitude of inferiority and bondage towards women. The biological weakness of a women makes her an easy prey particularly to physical domination. She is often a victim of physical violence not only outside her home but also in her come. Added to that the constant neglect of the female children, which apart from having adverse effect on their health also creates mental conditions for them in which they cannot resist any physical violence or several forms of injustices. They continue to be the weaker and the suppressed of the human species. What is, therefore, fundamentally necessary is to see that in matters of health and education they are treated at par with male children. Unless a beginning is thus made in every home in the early childhood of women, there are very few chances of their resisting the violence or not falling a prey to violence n society.

It is significant to note that only after the strong agitation by the women and the women's organisations there came substantial qualitative change in the law of sexual offences against women by the Criminal law Amendment act, 1983. Not only has the law been changed to punish the men guilty of the offence of rape more deterrently but it has also been moulded to see that the humiliation and shame of the victim is not compounded during or after the trial. The law has particularly been modified to provide the absence of true and genuine consent as the essential ingredient of the law of rape. Thus, the old law which very often permitted the accused to escape on the ground of apparent consent no longer holds the field. The minimum punishment for rape is laid down as seven years' imprisonment for ordinary cases but it is ten years' imprisonment in certain aggravated situations. There are seven such established aggravated situations set out in the new law. They refer to the custodial rape by (i) a public servant committing rape on a women in his custody by taking advantage of his official position; (ii) a police officer committing rape on a women in his custody; (iii) the manager of a jail, remand home or other place of detention, or a women's or children's institution committing rape on an inmate; and (iv) the manager of a hospital taking advantage of his official position and committing rape on "a woman in that hospital."

The other aggravated forms are where the victim is likely to be shocked by the rape, such as:

(i) rape on a woman under twelve years of age; and

(ii) a man committing rape on a woman knowing her to be pregnant;

(iii) 'gang rape'.

Section 114(A) in the evidence Act now provides for a conclusive presumption about absence of consent where sexual intercourse by the accused is proved and the victim states in her evidence before the Court that she did not consent.

The provision for holding the trail in camera and also preventing publication of its proceedings including the name of the victim except in law reports, is a salutary provision to protect the victim from further shame and humiliation.

As Indian society moves towards fuller development, it experiences some pulls and pushes. Some social problems emerge and some are accentuated. Among some of the pressing social problems facing the nation are those concerning children as they are the future of India. And, of course, one must ensure that one's future is safe, secure and in competent hands. Of the emerging social problems concerning children are single parent families, sexual abuse and disabled children. Problems that have been accentuated in the recent times are those of child labour and child prostitution. This chapter proposes to deal with each problem separately and to offer solutions in the same context.

Single Parenting

Most important reason for being a single parent is domestic incompatibility which could in extreme cases leads to separation/ divorce etc. Death of one parent or circumstances in which one parent has to be away constantly also leads to single parenting and deprives the child of a proper family environment. Single parenting has a direct impact on the concerned parent who faces hardships in managing a bouble role and in trying to compensate for the absent parent. Having a single parent also has a traumatic effect on the child who suffers from the apprehension of losing even the present parent.

Counsellors have generally been of the opinion that continuing domestic strife has an adverse impact on children and when this results in the children being to be in the custody of one parent, things do not improve, they can only become worse as a child needs both parents for a proper balancing and growth. Maternal love cannot take the place of absence of paternal love and vice versa. The advocates of divorce on the other hand, one of the opinion that it is better to have a single parents than have two engaged in constant bickersing resulting in chaos. The trauma of fighting parents is much worse. Therefore, the advocates of the divorce would find solace in watching a child grow in a peaceful environment with a single parent.

It is debatable whether single parent, due to death or due to marital strife is in any way different when looking after children. A single parent more often than no trends to become obsessive in the care of children so as to compensate for the absence of the other parent. This is an abnormal situation and can have nothing but abnormal results. This is not to say that children of single parent could not and do not grow-up to become responsible adults but they do so with greater difficulty. Because of the excessive love shown at times by the single parent children sometimes become very spoilt and difficult. Balancing of love and discipline become very difficult for a single parent because of time constraints and the fact that a child does need both parents for normal growth.

The problems of single parent becomes very much more acute with working single parent as they do not have as much time for their children as they would otherwise have had. The children have to be made conscious of money and the need for economy and the fact that the parent has to earn so as to help the family survive. This respect of work and of money is very important for a child as otherwise because of obsessive love of the single parent children sometimes show respect for neither. However, as far as possible, children should be taken out with the parents so as to make them to feel normal as compared to other children who go with both parents.

Since, a single parent family is among the most psychologically disturbed unit in any society some organisations should take up various support group for such units. In any case, these groups are constituted automatically as single parents do become interdependent on the parents of other children who are studying in the same schools/colleges as this involves sharing common transport, tuition and games, problems, etc. However, a structured system of assistance which gives more normalcy should be developed so as to give psychological and emotional support to such parents. Counselling can be a very useful aspect. Employment bureaus (part-time and full-time) would be very useful, particularly for single mothers. A structured system of assistance is yet to be worked out by any social organisation as single parent should develop some social and intellectual occupation outside the house so as to enable them to feel part of the mainstream.

Child Sexual Abuse

Child sexual abuse is considered to be a verbal or physical behaviour by one person (perpetuator) towards another person (victim), which is upsetting, demeaning, harmful and/or traumatic. Acts of child sexual abuse cover a whole range of misbehaviour from touching of private parts, making sexually gratifying remarks, showing pornographic photographs and films kissing to forcing the child to indulge in oral, anal and sexual intercourse.

Arbitrary estimates by experts claim that as many as three out of every five girls in our country are abused sexually. Shockingly 75 per cent of the sexual crime cases registered in India are against minors.

Why does sexual abuse of the child take place? No one can really tell. There are a host of reasons from which no one can make a generalisation. At the most one can try and list out the factors which aggravate the situation. One of the most important factors aggravating child sexual abuse is opportunity of being alone with the child. The second is accessibility to the child. The third is the kind of relationship the child shares with the offender. If the offender is a relative or lives in the same house there is greater chance of prolonged and secret abuse. The fourth reason could be open extra marital relationships of parents due to which the child loses his/her internal resistance to abnormal gestures. The fifth reason is high alcohol and drug consumption by parents in which case children have no role model to look up to. Lastly over crowding and abandonment also leads to child sexual abuse on the streets.

The offenders in the case of child sexual abuse are usually relatives from uncles, cousins and brothers-in-law. Friends, teachers and servants are also involves sometimes. The offenders gain pleasure and a sense of power from abuse. Some offenders are also psychopaths and drug and alcohol abusers.

Children who have been abused sexually usually keep the abuse a secret. But some behavioural are physical disorders indicate that a child may have been abused sexually. These disorders are bedwetting, violent dreams, significant drop in school performance, depression, self-destructive behaviour, running away, knowledge of sexual matters inappropriate to age, acting infantile fears, and probias, pain during urination, sore or swollen genital areas, extreme feeling of guilt and shame and anorexia.

Unfortunately there is no specific law that deals with child sexual abuse adequately. It is usually taken up under the rape law, i.e. Section 376 of the IPC and sometimes under Section 377 of the IPC which criminalises 'unnatural' sexual offences. Further, more the Indian law allows rape of minors within marriage. Therefore, we need separate laws to deal with child sexual abuse.

To help children affected by child sexual abuse, the victim must be removed from the vicinity of the abuser at once. Communication—helping the child to express his/her feelings is also successful. The child should be taught to assert herself/himself and such children should also be given proper support and treatment. Sexual education should also be encouraged in schools. To conclude I would say that keeping children safe is most important. The child should be taught about 'good' and 'bad' touches. Listening to your child daily and being caring and involved with 'your child helps in averting the situations leading to sexual abuse of the child.

Child Disability

Among some of the emerging social problems facing children today are those emanating from impairments, disability and handicaps. Impairment means any loss or abnormality of psychological, physiological or anatomical structure or function. Disability relates to any restriction or lack (resulting from an impairment) of ability to perform an activity in the manner or within the range considered normal for a human being. Handicap means a disadvantage for a given individual resulting from an impairment or a disability that limits or prevents the fulfillment of a role that is normal (depending on age, sex and social and cultural factors) for that individual.

The following types of disabling conditions may be found

among children everywhere:

(a) Children considered to be severely mentally impaired, deficient or retarded.

(b) Child considered to be slow learners.

(c) Children considered to have speech or language defects.

(d) Children with hearing impairments.

(e) Children who are blind.

(f) Children who are partially sighted.

(g) Children who are motor handicapped.

(h) Children with specific types of learning disabilities.

(i) Children who have behavioural problems, are maladjusted and psychotic.

(j) Children with various combinations of such conditions.

It is disturbing to note that in 1975 there were 516 million disabled people and it is estimated that by the year 2000 there will be at least 774 million disabled people in the world. It has also been estimated that the annual growth rate of disabled people is 1.63 per cent. However, tragically some of these disabilities can be prevented by full coverage of pregnant women by maternal and child services, legislation, education, attitude changes, etc. However, sometimes it is an act of god and must be accepted as such. The tragedy of the disabled child is that the parents of the child become over protective and the child is completely paralysed and removed from the society. The society in turn also looks down upon the child with sympathy and/or indifference. So the disabled child becomes an unproductive and complex burden on society. The child himself/herself starts to feel useless and an object of pity.

Here society must intervene. Rehabilitation of such children is a must so that they can became a productive and useful part of society. For this it is necessary that

(a) there is identification of children with impairments.

(b) there should be direction or co-ordination of service delivery.

(c) medical care and treatment, including the provision of prosthetic and prosthetic appliances.

(d) vocational assessment, training and placement.

(e) social counselling and assistance.

(f) provision of technical aids and appliances.

The mass media can also help the disabled by attempting to create public awareness of the rights of the disabled, making parents aware of the importance of early detection of disability and to help them accept it where it exits, presenting a special news edition for the handicapped involving handicapped, in the planning of their own media programmes, mobilising government institutions, local government and other agencies in this effort through workshops, seminars, etc., ensuring co-ordination through creation of a permanent co-ordinating committee among governmental agencies, NGOs and the mass media, and stressing involvement of disabled children in arts, sports, social affairs, etc., and urging sports clubs, youth centres and educational institutions to offer appropriate aid and facilities to such children.

Child Labour

Accentuation of the problem of child labour throughout the world is a result of globalisation. In India child labour is a national tragedy. International Organisations (such as the ILO and UNICEF) along with child rights activities, human rights groups and governments are joining hands to eliminate child labour. Extreme difficulty is faced in estimating the number of child labourers in the world. However, according to the ILO almost 250 million children in the age group of 5-14 are working in the developing countries. In India 12.7 million children are full time child workers and 10.5 million are marginal child workers.

The supporters of child labour are resistant to change and offer several arguments in favour of child labour. First, they say that if the child does not work he/she will starve. This is not true as children can avoid starvation by working a few hours a day. But they are made to work 8 to 10 hours a day and in human conditions and paid half the amount paid to an adult. The second argument is that if stopped from working they will move to a more degrading industry—the sex industry. This again is extremely unlikely if the governments joint together to ban child labour. The sex industry is not as profitable as many of the export industries where child labour is in practice. This kind of labour is more visible as it requires indentifiable locations and is easier to target. The third argument is that children have always worked in the industry of traditional handicrafts and the developed nations do not understand that these industries will die if children do not learn the skill. This again is not true because children were part of the labour force in artisanal and agricultural economies but it was within their families and the workload allowed time for play and interaction with other children. Today, however, children work away from their families to toil in illegal factories. The small children who work in inhuman conditions are not furthering the cause of traditional handicraft but are being exploited to meet international competition and demand for cheap goods.

In India, children are working the industries of slate, pencil, diamond cutting, agate cutting, gem polishing, powerlom, cotton hosiery, carpet weaving, lock making, pottery, brassware, match, glass, silk and silk products, textile, knives, handicrafts, silk weaving, brocade and zari and in brick kilns. As a result they suffer from diseases like asthma, chronic bronchitis, tuberculosis, eye defects, stunted growth, tetnus, skin diseases and silicosis.

The reasons why children are pushed into working at a very young age are exploitation of poverty, the absence of education and the restrictions of tradition. Poverty of course is the most powerful force driving children to work in hazardous industries. For poor families the small contribution of a child's income or assistance at home makes the difference between hunger and bare sufficiency. Survey after survey makes this very clear. Exploitation of the poor is a vicious circle poverty begets child labour be gets lack of education that eventually begets poverty gain. Lack of relevant education has hit children particularly hard. Education in India is clearly under funded and whatever funds there are, are misused. The school system therefore is adversely affected. Moreover schools in India are often rigid and uninspiring in approach, promoting a curriculum that is irrelevant to remote from the children's lives. The quality of teaching is abysmally low and the discipline violent. So it creates an unwillingness among the children as well as the parents to send the child to school. Tradition and social patterns also play an important part in forcing children to work. Traditionally it was thought that work was the most effective way of teaching children about life and the world. The residue of this notion still remains. The rigidity of the caste system in India is such that although the dominant cultural group may not wish its own children to work but it will not be so concerned if young people from racial, ethnic or economic minorities do it. And as traditional forces push children into work, the situation is worsened by the growing culture of consumerism.

Ending Child Labour

Since the causes of child labour are complex and include poverty, economic exploitation, social values and cultural circumstances, solutions must be comprehensive and must involve the widest range of partners in each society. Some specific actions that need to be taken up urgently are as follows: hazardous and exploitative forms of child labour including bonded labour that hampers the child's physical, social, cognitive, emotional and moral development must not be tolerate and the government and voluntary organisations must take immediate steps to end them. The governments must fulfill their responsibility to make relevant primary education free and compulsory for all children and ensure that all children attend primary school on a full time basis. Governments must budget the necessary resources for this purpose with donors ensuring adequate resources from existing development aid budgets.

Although the Supreme Court of India on the 10th of December 1996 issued a judgement in the best interest of child labour, there are still some loopholes left. Laws on child labour and education should be consistent in purpose and implemented in a mutually supportive way National child labour laws must accord with both the spirit and letter of the relevant ILO conventions. Such legislation must encompass the vast majority of child work in the informal sector of the economy, including work on the streets and farms, domestic work or work of the child within his/her own household.

All children should be registered at birth. Registration is essential to permit exercise of the child rights such as access to education, health care and other services. It also provides employers and labour inspectors with evidence of every child's age.

Since data on child labour is scarce, national and international systems must be put in place to gather and analyse comparable data on child labour. This would ensure that the problem is addressed effectively. Special attention should be given to the forgotten or 'invisible' children working as domestic servants on family farms.

The codes of conduct and procurement policies of national and international corporations should be urged to adopt codes of conduct guaranteeing that neither they or their sub-contractors will employ children in conditions that violates their rights. Governments all over the world should refuse to buy products from any supplier that exploits children.

Child Prostitution

There is no point in emphasizing that child prostitution is bad and degrading. However, sexual exploitation of children is increasing in all over the world. The underground nature of the multi-billion dollar illegal industry of commercial sexual exploitation of children make it difficult to gather reliable data. According to a UNICEF report more than two million children throughout the world are being sexually abused. Girls are being forced into this hazardous form of labour and boys are often exploited also. Most of the children are being used for prostitution and pronography child sex abuse has almost always been identified with underdeveloped countries, especially South-East Asia, but widespread child prostitution exists even in the industrialized countries. Foreign tourists have especially been attracted by inexpensive sex workers. A report states that the number of child prostitutes in India in 1994 was three lakhs and by 1995 it had increased to 5 lakhs. This increase of about 50 per cent in just one year is indeed shameful.

There are two aspects to child prostitution. One is the demand side and the other is the supply side. First, we shall analyse the demand side. The demand for child prostitution emanates basically from perversion. This perversion again depends on lack of education and the family and/or the social background, which distorts the moral code of the people who come in its purview. Apart from perverts, the demand for child prostitution also comes from psychopaths, truck drivers and similar people, tourists and mostly people away from home. A severe malady, out of lack of regular sexual behaviour also causes demand for child prostitution. Recently however it has also been observed that old people and people who do not have the confidence to approach a growth up woman/man for sex are also demanding child prostitution. In addition to people who actually buy sex, there are traffickers, agents and intermediaries who profit from the sale of children. There are entrepreneurs who organise sex tours or who produce brochures encouraging the notion that young girls or boys are sexually available.

On the other hand, the supply of child prostitutes comes from the following poverty, homelessness, professional criminals and syndicates who run brothels and profit from child prostitution, kidnap and abduct young girls or lure them and, a naturally promiscuous nature. However, the last factor is an extreme rarity. The regular sex worker should be contrasted with a child prostitute because a regular sex worker can be driven not only by need for money but also because of sexual appetite. However in the case of a child the latter is not true. Thus poverty is one major cause fueling supply. A heavily distorted moral code also gives a fillip to the supply of child prostitutes. This is amply visible in countries like Bangladesh, Thailand and Vietnam. Global market forces have also contributed to the supply of child prostitution by widening the gap between the rich and poor-encouraging migration, destabilishing families destroying support systems and safety nets. Conflicts and wars also create conditions in which children are sexually exploited.

Having analysed both the demand and supply side of child prostitution we now can pinpoint some solutions to the problem. The supply of child prostitution can be curtailed by proper education to parents as well as children. Awareness must be created about the issue and children should be properly protected by state intervention. The demand for child prostitution can be choked of with the help of education and counselling. NGOs being local people can play important role in this respect. They can also help in reforming distorted moral codes existing in their areas of operation. The majesty, might and money of the government can also ensure convergence and orchestration of all efforts to attain social justice and remove its evils despite constraints of politics and insensitivity.

As regards Suppression of Immoral Traffic Act it is well known that the institution of prostitution was legalized in our country mainly because of this occupation of the British Army. Te British army in India consisted both of Indian and British soldiers. The military authorities provided Indian prostitutes for the soldiers, in effect running a system of licensed prostitution which included registration, compulsory medical examination and hospital treatment if necessary, a sliding tariff according to the soldier's rank, and some times even provision of accommodation. In 1884 the Quartermaster General wrote that special quarters meant that "the women can be well –managed and easily found for examination and... the soldiers know where to go as soon as they arrive at the station." The Indian Contagious diseases Act of 1968, following the English legislation, had regularized these provisions. The same thing is true of the American army. When they left Thailand after the Second World War, it left behind over half a million unmarried girls present and since then the profession of prostitution thrived in Thailand.

In India it was much later in 1954 tat a serious attempt was

Table 1: Number of Victims of Rape by Age Group, States and Major Cities, 1994

States	*No. of Cases reported*	*Number of Victims Aged*			
		Below 10 years	*10-16 Years*	*16-30 Years*	*Above 30 years*
Andhra Pradesh	873	72	288	433	80
Aurnachal Pradesh	28	5	12	11	0
Assam	530	23	119	308	80
Bihar	1130	15	198	722	195
Delhi	309	54	146	98	16
Goa	8	1	2	5	1
Gujarat	356	20	93	186	57
Haryana	258	29	90	114	25
Himachal Pradesh	110	9	30	61	10
Jammu & Kashmir	109	3	2	72	35
Karnataka	281	27	72	161	21
Kerala	197	9	53	115	20
Madhya Pradesh	2929	97	712	1680	440
Maharashtra	1304	92	399	705	108
Manipur	5	1	0	2	2
Meghalaya	34	0	7	24	3
Mizoram	44	2	15	23	4
Nagaland	12	0	0	10	2
Orissa	436	14	66	288	68
Punjab	108	8	34	52	14
Rajasthan	1002	76	129	644	153
Sikkim	9	3	1	4	1
Tamil Nadu	237	9	23	179	26
Tripura	61	1	12	32	16
Uttar Pradesh	2078	71	467	1205	335
West Bengal	743	89	270	302	82
Andaman Nicobar Islands	4	1	0	2	2

Chandigarh	6	2	1	1	2
Dadra and Nagar Haveli	2	0	0	1	0
Daman and Diu	1	0	0	1	0
Lakshadweep	0	0	0	0	0
0					
Pandicherry	4	1	2	1	0
Total	13208	734	3244	7442	1798
Some Major Cities					
Ahmedabad	20	5	10	0	5
Bangalore	61	4	27	28	2
Bhopal	62	4	18	23	17
Calcutta	36	4	14	15	3
Chennai	14	1	5	8	0
Coimbatore	1	0	0	1	0
Delhi	252	44	116	83	12
Hyderabad	49	9	15	22	3
Indore	29	3	9	12	5
Jaipur	22	1	5	11	5
Kanpur	31	3	9	12	7
Kochi	7	0	0	6	1
Lucknow	33	3	11	14	5
Ludhiana	11	1	5	2	3
Madurai	4	0	0	4	0
Mumbai	150	32	57	54	7
Nagpur	46	5	13	23	5
Patna	25	0	0	20	4
Pune	52	1	25	22	4
Surat	10	2	6	2	0
Vadodara	13	1	3	4	5
Varanasi	9	0	2	3	4
Visakhapatnam	21	1	5	15	0

Source: Crime in India. 1994, National Crime Records Bureau

made to curtail the exploitation of women for the purposes of prostitution and the Suppression of Immoral Traffic Act in women and girls was brought on the Statute Book. Your discussion on this topic will expose the weaknesses and infirmities in the Statute and also make suggestions for improving the same. Today, with existence of destitute conditions for women and illiteracy and neglect,.

Table 2: Incidence of Crimes Against Women by Crime Head 1990-94

Crime Head	*Year*					*Percentage Variation in 1994*	
	1990	*1991*	*1992*	*1993*	*1994*	*1990*	*1993*
Rape	9,518	9,793	11,112	11,242	12351	29.8	9.9
Kidnapping and Abduction	11,899	12,300	12,077	11,837	12998	11.1	--
Dowry Deaths	4,836	5,157	4,962	5,817	4935	2.0	-15.2
Torture	13,450	15,949	19,750	22,064	25946	92.9	17.6
Molestation	20,194	20,611	20,385	20,985	24117	19.4	14.9
Sexual Harassament	8,620	10,283	10,751	12,009	10496	21.8	-12.6
Importation of Girls	--	--	--	--	167	--	--
Immoral Traffic (Prevention) act	--	--	--	--	7547	--	--
Indecent Representation	--	--	--	--	389	--	--
Total crime against women	69,317	74,093	79,037	83,954	98,948	45.0	17.9
Percentage to total IPC crimes	4.3	4.4	4.7	5.2	5.6		

women are an easy prey for being exploited for prostitution. This can be seen against the background of past experience in our country so far as the child widows were concerned. Many high caste widows, especially child widows, were either abandoned, or subject to such abuse that they were forced to leave home. Most of these girls and women had not alternative but to support themselves through prostitution. Kamaladevi Chattopadhyay reports a study by amrita Pal in 1869 which found that 90% of prostitutes were widows, many of whom were Brahmins. It was left to social reformers like Pandita Ramabai to improve the position of widows in the 19th century. It in the back ground of this exploitation that one finds it surprising that SITA does not punish a man for indulging in prostitution.

Since the man is really the active agent in the process of prostitution, the law should be so amended to make the sentence more deterrent for a man who indulges in prostitution. What is necessary for this purpose is that the investigation of these offences should be entirely done by the women wing of the police and should not be kept in the hands of the male police.

REFERENCES

Burra Neera, *Born to Work: Child Labour in India*, Oxford University Press, New Delhi 1995

Rai Usha, *Life in the Right Track Parenting*, January, 1997.

Ray, Dunu, *Rights of Child Labour*, Ethics: Production and Nationwide Economic & Political weekly, January 31, 1998.

CHAPTER 2

Marriage and Dowry: A Social Perspective

Dowry is the most common social evil that cause crimes against women in India. In this materialistic age even rich, elite and enlightened people are badly engrossed with the idea of Dowry. If marriage is a necessary institution dowry is also unavoidable. Dowry is anything given in cash or kind to the son-in-law and to his parents before, during, or, after the marriage. If unfulfilled, it may led to harassment or pressures on the bride and her family. Dowry does not merely mean what is given at the time of marriage. It often includes the enormous expenses incurred on travel, entertainment of the bridgegroom's party, and the conduct of public ceremony. In the first few years of marriage, the bride's treatment in her husband's house depends on how much she was given and how much she is expected to bring. Thus, dowry is not an isolated payment but an array of gifts given over a time. But, what is more important is what is given at the time of marriage, which constitutes the major portion of dowry. The education, economic independence and selfesteem of the girl is given secondary importance to amassing he dowry required for her marriage.

Rajaraman (1983) considers dowry to be a compensation for the lower economic value of women not working or employed. Dowry as a monetary compensation for the maintenance of the girl is not on par with the productive and reproductive contribution that her subsistence would cost the household, she marries into. Dowry harassment and deaths are indicators of the low status of women in India, it is an all pervasive, deep-rooted and age old custom. In India dowry has been a persistent problem. It has deeply demoralized the position of women in the society, lowered her prestige and dignity, much more than any other social phenomenon in India. Recently, the deaths of women in the forms of strangulation, committing culpable homicide, ill-treatment, physical violence and mental harassment leading to suicide, all these for not bringing sufficient dowry are commonly noticed and reported in the newspapers.

The women has now become a commodity to be sold and bought in the marriage market. She has been reduced to a mere saleable commodity. In fact, dowry has now taken on such malignant proportions that it has corrupted the very fabric of family and society in India. Al norms and values are virtually thrown to the wind when the proposal for marriage for girls arises, and it is money that solely guides the human conscience in setting up human relations and families.

Tracing its evolution, dowry in any form was not sanctioned by the ancient Hindu religious scriptures (Palu, 1986) Sreedhan (Wife's property) has been a vital aspect of marriage of higher castes/classes of women. The classical notion of streedhan is no longer applied in the modern context. Dowry today refers to a large cash transaction made by the bride's parents to the bridegroom and his parents which includes gifts, cash, ornaments and so on. The practice of dowry is spreading mainly because of four reasons. First, whatever is transferred as Streedhan at the time of marriage is taken away by the bridegroom and his kins. Second, the cash transacted is nowhere mentioned in the Brahminical dictum. Third, the bridegroom's parents to whom the cash passes, utilize it to purchase husbands for their own daughters. Fourth, the demand for more dowry continues even after marriage.

During the Vedic period, in many cases, men and women enjoyed equal opportunities in education and work. In the post-Vedic period, this view was totally distorted ad broken, and replaced by the patriarchical domination ideology (Madhavananda and Majumdar 1953. Chatterjee, 1974) which gave authority to the husband/male over the wife/female. Thus, segregation came into existence. The women was usually viewed and accepted as a daughter, a wife and a mother. Her role and position were sub-ordinated to the ale in the family as well as in the society. This had its sanction from Manu. The system of Kanyadan (gift of virgin) was probably the outcome of this, dominant Brahminical patriarchical ideology. Classical literature is full of instances of Kanyadan among the upper castes and the propertied classes who transferred not only daughters but also movable as well as immov-able properties (Kapadia 1906, Karve 1953). The dakshina given to the bridegroom was prescribed by the Shastrakaras. The quan-tum however depended on one's social status and wealth. The Dharmasastras also recommended dakshina to the bridge as streedhan (wife's property) over which she enjoyed complete legal rights.

In fact, the main idea behind the Streedhan was to provide her economic security to meet any unforeseen eventuality in her life, like death of her husband or desertion (Ray, 1985). Yet another idea was to make the couple lead a happy and comfortable life without facing any problem. In this case, she had complcte legal rights over her Streedhan as recommended by dharmasastras. Thus, these brahminical cultural elaborations tried to mould the whole society according to this world-view (Bhowmick, 1984). How-ever, this idea of cultural elaborations or beliefs to a severe set-back in the colonia era. As the time passed, many powerful and dominant castes resorted to the phypergamous kanyadan marriage in order to attract the desirable bridegrooms, for their daughters. Thus, with deviation came the possession of wealth and power among the upper castes which became a convention. But 'dowry' a modification term for streedhan became a recent modern phe-nomenon, especially after World War II with a new meaning and purpose (Rose 1961, Srinivas, 1984). The new socio-economic forces; modernisation colonial education system have brought new cleavages in the social structure. The fostering of new values (for example, measuring of status in terms of money, power, and the like) have distorted the whole traditional system without changing the concept of kayadan and varadakshina. Consequently, a new meaning has come about for dowry.

The new values of status-acquisition and achievement in life have distorted the letter and spirit of streedhan. It is this that has brought cataclysmic changes in social distinctions and class structure which in turn fostered the evil to acquire new dimension. It has brought changes in the system and position of women. Naturally, women in general, particularly from non-affluent castes/ classes have become victims to this obnoxious, development in socio-economic structure. It is this hunt of 'suitable' and 'desirable' husbands which has driven the bride's parents to acquire wealth indiscriminately and use it for marriage purposes. Thus, in a way, parents with their illusions and delusions have contributed to the growth of dowry as an evil. From the foregoing observations, it may be concluded that it is a logical attempt to legitimize the avarice of some social classes of people by "linking it up with an ancient and respected custom" in transitional Indian Society.

Perpetuation of Dowry

The custom of dowry in marriage was absent in the past. Instead, streedhan (wife's property) was predominant in a kanyadan (giving away of a daughter) form of Brama marriage. Such a form of marriage practiced even today is the reserve of a person of good pedigree and equipped with coverable qualifications (Madan, 1975, Srinivas, 1984).

Admittedly, before 'dowry' had come into existence, in the ancient marriage customs bridge price' or bride wealth prevailed. The giftsmade to the bride' skin in exchange for the bride is commonly known as the 'ride-price.' This custom has been replaced by 'dowry' in several parts of this country particularly amongst the tribal communities in Tamil Nadu, Kerala, Orissa, Bihar, Karnataka. Rajsthan (Krishnamurthy, 1981). Among these tribal groups, in exchange for the bride it is customary to pay in cash or kind and hence, it is known as the 'bride-price.' Some communities give goats and cattle, while some give clothes, ornaments, tools and implements, liquor and grain and other items. On receipt of the bride-price, the bride's father parts with his daughter and also his authority over her is transferred to the bridegroom. In implies a compensation given to the bride's father for parting with his daughter. Whatever the custom, which prevailed or is prevailing the quantum of bride-price also has a direct bearing on the status of the bride-price also ha a direct bearing on the status of the bride after her marriage.

It has been observed that many families have been caught in financial problems due to changes in the social scene. The compulsions of the economic necessities and the race towards materialism have forced a large number of communities and sub-castes which were practicing 'bridge-price' to switch over to the custom of 'dowry'. It may how how-ever be noticed that in both the bride-price and dowry customs, there is the transmission of property. Both have adverse impact on the social status of women. It is difficult to define and clarify the concept of dowry. Even the Government of India in its Dowry Prohibition act of 1961, which was later amended in 1984, has not clarified as to what exactly constitutes 'dowry'. According to the present practice dowry usually subsumes material gifts and cash paid to the bridegroom and his kin. This is down not only before and at the time of marriage but also even after the marriage (Paul, 1992).

The commonest items included in dowry are jewels clothes and other household and luxury goods like refrigerator and kitchen utensils. These are ideally trested as the bride's streedhan (wife's property). It also includes gifts for the son-in-law and other luxury items like scooter or car, VCR, gifts for the bridegroom's parents and other relatives. Over and above this, it includes hard cash, paid as contribution towards the marriage expenses (Dube, 1983). In some cases, dowry is also paid as compensation for the expenditure incurred for the education and further training of the groom. This money is usually kept with the bridegroom's parents (Sharma, 1980). It may be noted here that the bride does not have any rights over the properly that she brings and gives to her bridgegroom at the time of marriage.

Thus, she has virtually forfeited all legal rights unless specified and sanctioned by the court in respect of Dowry Prohibition Act. Further, besides the gifts offered to the bridgegroom, the bride's parents have to bear the marriage expenses, spend money in such a way that befits their social and economic status (Vatuk, 1975).

Actually the system of dowry has strengthened the patriarchy in the contemporary Indian Society among all religious communities (Upadhya, 1990, Paul, 1987). This is turn has lowered the status of women in the family and society as well. Subjugation of women, according her a secondary place in the home, ill-treatment, perpetuating inequality by exploiting her for selfish causes have resulted in lowering her position and status in the society. Tough the age-old custom has its won social and religious sanction, it has become a means for satisfying the greed of people in this increasingly materialistic world.

Dowry and Violence

Coming to pernicious results of dowry, usually, for not bringing dowry, violence is resorted to by males towards their women partners. This takes place after marriage. The violence may be in any form leading to the death of a women. Dowry deaths are increasing day by day despite stringent laws, police action and social movements. All India statistics show that the dowry deaths have risen from 386 in 1983 to 1912 in 1987, 2209 in 1988 3829 in 1989 and 4006 in 1990 (Police records, Ministry of Home Affairs, Government of India, compendium of Policy statements in Parliament Budget session 1990, Rajya Sabha). Dowry deaths were reported to be 4.46 in 1987, 5.99 in 1988 and 6.9 per cents in 1989. Further, it has been reported that in every four hours there is one dowry death in the country. Statewise breakup of dowry deaths for the year 1989 shows the U.P. ranks first with 1364 deaths. Maharashtra second with 690 deaths and Wet Bengal third with 402 deaths (women's Link,1993).

In all the Cases of dowry deaths, the victims are invariably women who are young with hardly any education and no secure employment. Tehmajority of victims are below 25 years of age which shows tht harassment must have begin early, within seven years of marriage, a period which has legal sanction. The common modes of deaths are burning alive (by pouring kerosene), consuming poison, hanging, drowning, murders and suicides. A greater number of cases reported are of murders and suicides. What is significant is that the majority of the cases, nearly 80 per cent of them have taken place in urban areas. Only a few cases are reported from rural areas. These deaths seem to be a 'city-phenomenon'. The reasons for this phenomenon maybe due to growing commercialization of living standards, developing new appetites for luxurious consumer goods, rise in cost of living, economic marginalisation of he lower income groups and a tendency to improve their social status in competition with other prosperous communities and families. This trend illustrates the position and place of women in the society. Despite modern civilization education and exposure to media, it is a proven fact that the impact of these aspects on men and women is of little significance.

The evil has spread to all sections in the society. Further, the system of dowry has penetrated many patriarchal tribals/peasants like those in Arunachal Pradesh and Himachal Pradesh (government of India, 1974). The interplay of precapitalist values and modern forces with the accentuation of the free market economy and the consumer culture have contributed to the promotion of dowry. Women have become double victims of the traditional and modern...socio-political and economic systems. Earlier, they were not encouraged to participate in the economic activity outside their household and now they are locked up in a society based on unequal development which can generate jobs only for a few. Thus, the limited enclave type of modern development and the infusion of the culture of aggressive consumerism without fair distributive justice, have characteristically made most of the families of non-affluent sections suffer while arranging marital alliances. Now the nature of dowry is governed by both socio-cultural and economic factors. Te latter is being increasingly resorted to in a society which appreciates false prestige and status measured in terms of wealth also (Mandal, 1984). Material considerations like wealth, type of profession, status of the family and prestige are some of the qualifications that get predominance in the establishment of any marital alliance between two families (Paul, 1986).

About the then position of dowry, Altekar (1938) reports "it was a matter of preserving the status of a daughter as well as son. Sons might inherit all the productive capacity but the daughters had to be assured of the same (or better) standard of life to which they were accustomed". In spite of laws, press reports, social awareness and the social movements, dowry persists. It is all pervasive and has become a necessary evil in all families and communities. The quantum varies from family to family depending upon their status. The pressures so exerted are certainly not in consonance with the actual wealth of the parents of the parents of the bride. As a result, many middle class families are forced into economic debts and problems. Over the years the ramifications of dowry have reached unimaginable proportions. Altekar, (1938) observes that the recent trends in dowry have proved to be highly disasterous. Despite tremendous changes in the social sphere, dowry has begun to assume scandalous proportions and the menance has spread to all corners of the country and percolated into several communities.

Dowry and Status of Women

Dowry and status of women are interlinked There is an affinity between the two, and the former has its impact and influence upon the latter. The truth, however, is that dowry has adversely affected the status and position of women in the society. It has lowered and degraded the position of women. It has corrupted and demoralized women. Variables like education and occupation have little or non influence on the status of women. In other words, the notion that it, women are educated and are in better position in occupational structure the quantum of dowry is not necessary, has been dispelled. The phenomenon of dowry is not altogether absent when the women are financially independent (Paul 1986) It is one's socio-economic status that aids and perpetuates dowry. In this situations she has to take heavy dowry with her to minimize her with her dependency status. This degraded position makes them utilize the system of dowry to overcome their disadvantaged position.

The modern socio-economic forces have given a different meaning to the purpose of marriage among the people in different socio-economic strata. The sole concern of parents seems to be to pursue their pecuniary interests in the making of marital alliance. In fact, some women also support and encourage this pattern of marriage.

The prevailing economic and social effects of the marriage are greater among the less affluent segments than among the more affluent sections of society. The real victims are from the lower classes and lower castes. The upper castes somehow get on with the custom. The poor sections imitate the upper castes and hence the victims are invariably poor, innocent women. Further, the, dominant patriarchal values are instilled among the daughters during the socialization process. For example, marriage without dowry is not considered marriage at all. Thus a sense of competition has entered the marital arena. This, has encouraged certain sections to make easy money through the manipulation of marriage alliances. Also the black and unaccounted money plays an important role in ostentatious marriages and limits the marital prospects of some good and talented women of limited financial means. The problem of dowry is not solely that of the younger persons but also that of their old parents whole are burdened with the feudal and traditional ideas of getting, 'desirable,' suitable, husbands for their daughters.

Impact of Dowry

The evil effects of dowry are many. They system affect not only individuals especially women and their parents but family, society and nation as well. This mainly affect the middle classes and poor sections of h society who wish to get their daughters married. It lowers the prestige and status of women in the society. What is distressing to be noted in human relations is that it has replaced the harmonious relationship between husband and wife, the warmth and affection and love are ruled by the factor of money. In the majority of cases money binds the husband; and wife together. Dowry causes late marriages. Because of these late marriages many women after crossing a particular age remain to be spinsters. They hardly develop the inclination to get married, in other words, this invariably leads to the development of an version and hatred towards men. Further, this results is emotional maladjustments and imbalances in their perceptions and understanding of human problem. Another evil effect is that parents from lower strata in order to see that their daughter s are wedded to desirable men, seek to get money from other sources by some means or the other. This creates indebtedness among them which becomes a social stigma, if they are unable to repay the debts.

Usually, after marriage the in-laws and husbands force the women to get more money from their parents in order to fulfill their monstrous needs and requirements. When they fail to get the money demanded by their husbands, the latter fail to get the money demanded by their husbands, the latter harass the former. This results in depression and frustration and mental agony which drive the women to commit suicide.

One more evil effect of dowry is that it has created a great gap between the rich and the poor. Class distinction and caste differences persists. The boys also suffer when the parents do not allow them to many girls whom they like. For want of more dowry as compensation for what they invested on education, the parents force their sons to marry girls whose parents offer ore dowry. As a result, a great misunderstanding is created between the parents and their sons, between husbands and wives. It destroy marital peace and the home can no longer be a place of succour and comfort to he women. And children born out of such tense wedlocks growing under such conditions would be unhealthy and abnormal.

The compulsions surely breed corruption which not only affects the family but the society as a whole. It infuses the blood of black and unaccounted money which in turn may affect the nations' economy. The pompous way of conducting marriage and the lavish spendings are unnecessary wasteful expenditure which generates inflation which normally affect the common man. Perpetuation of this custom has created an evil thought that the birth of a girl in a family is a liability and hence it is treated with apprehension and unhappiness. Dowry as a custom is a violation of all the egalitarian concept and is a certain obstruction to the goals of national construction. It is self-defeating and suicidal in every sense if it is perpetrated further. Further, it has caused the development of many lopsided social values leading to social tensions. It is an anthema to the sacred ideals of social and economic justice enshrined in the Constitution of India. It has forced women to accept her unenviable position meekly and her individuality is greatly destroyed.

Dowry Prohibition (Amended) Act, 1984: A Critique

Dowry has become a social evil, an incorrigible obstancle for imparting social justice. It is an anathema to the progress and all round development of women' personality. It is and all round development of women's personality. It is now institutionalized a right to be demanded by the boys' parents. While the necessity to fight against this evil and eradicate it has been promoted by many social reformers and activists, the movement has finally culminated in the enactment of dowry Prohibition Act, 1961. But this legal battle as the present trend shows has failed to combat the most dreaded evil. Despite law and social outcry, dowry still persists either in subtle or overt from making the life of both parents and the girls miserable beyond measure.

The low status accorded to women which has its social, religious sanctions has been one of the important reasons for the subjugation and exploitation of women in various facets of our social life. This low status attributed to her has contributed to the emergence of several invidious and antisocial customs like infanticide, child marriage, dowry and so on which has affected the very women hood itself (Krishamurthy, 1981). This was first recognized by the great social reformers like Raja Ram Mohan

Roy, Tilak, Ramakrishna, Swami Vivekananda and a score of others who made relentless crusade against the evil practice being perpetrated against women. Later, this movement was strongly supported and promoted by Mahatma Gandhi and other leaders who described the inequity between men and women. The resurgent social values so ennobled by these great individuals have been well reflected in the Constitution of India. The preamble f the constitution speaks and emphasizes about a society in which women are equal to men in all respects and the people are assured of justice-social, economic and political.

The dowry problem had drawn the attention of social thinkers, reformers and legal men only in the beginning of Twentieth century. The results of their struggles is the enactment of Dowry Prohibition Act of 1961 and this legislation came into force from 1st July. 1961. This act consists of ten sections. All these sections deal with definition and nature, territorial extent of its own application, punishment and the competent court to try, the offence. We must remember that until 1975 the dowry was not made a cognizable offence. Only a few cases were recorded and pending in the court all over India. This was confirmed by the Committee on the Status of Women in 1975 when it toured the whole country which later recommended that the laws must be made stringent and forcible. Even though only four cases were prosecuted in 1974 and a dozen cases registered in 1975, the horrendous nature of dowry, its evil effects could not be ruled out. The persistence of the cruel custom continued despite the law.

The reasons for the non-performance of the Act of 1961 were quite obvious. The act itself was full of shortcomings. It failed to equip itself to deal with the cases of dowry deaths. A careful scrutiny of the Act would make us understand how effective and stringent the law must have been in order to combat the evil on the legal front. One thing was sure that the act failed to achieve the objects for which it was conceived. Among the reasons the Act itself has rendered infirm with too many escape-routes and has thus enabled social recalcitrants to violate the dowry law with impugnity. Another reasons lies in the lack of social support for the law. Social apathy and community indifference clearly reflected in inadequate social involvement in the implementation of the law. Hypocrisy was practiced by people, while they condemned it on the one hand and on the other they widely accepted it, thus the pernicious evil has been promoted and natured. Further, the dowry death were not strongly condemned and the persons involved net denounced. The perpetrators of crime were accepted as common citizens and they were encouraged in fresh matrimonial alliances.

Another important reasons to be attributed to the failure of the Act is that there are many shortcomings and inadequacies in eh strategies of enforcement. Lack of political will and lack of zeal on the part o people have severely strained the implementation of the law. These shortcomings have made the law weak and ineffective. In spite of the drawback, the fact may be noted that if the existing law itself is strictly enforced by the police as well as the bureaucrats, the menace may be contained to some extent. We have umpteen laws. What is lacking is the responsibility and accountability on the part of legal machinery to enforce the law Therefore, what is needed is not the addition of amendments which are so warranted, but the commitment and sincerity in implementing the existing laws.

implementing the laws he onerous responsibility also lies on the shoulders of bureaucracy which is the vehicle for running the administration of the country smoothly. It is one thing to enact laws favouring the oppressed and the suppressed and quite another to implement them at various levels with political zeal and sagacity so as to bring succour to the actual victims and make the transformation a reality. And for the proper conditions to be ensured, the law makers, enacters and enforcers should come together with a will to tackle the problem of dowry on all fronts. Otherwise, the symbolic relationship between the dowry and the status of Indian women continues to be mockery in the eyes of every one. Besides, the laws referring to marriage, divorce, abortion, maintenance, inheritance, matrimonial property and so forth are also to be strengthened. The spate of reforms and amendments are commendable.

Everybody expresses his/her concern with the way the police functions while dealing with the dowry death cases. The approach of police with regard to the cases of dowry is somewhat casual, lackadaisical and sometimes callous and indifferent. This attitude has to be shed and the police must ac dispassionately and deligently without preconceived prejudices. In order to translate the laws into a meaningful reality, it is absolutely essential for the police to play a greater role in checking the abuse of law wit aright understanding of the issues involved and with some amount of sensitivity.

Laws alone cannot be sufficient to eradicate or minimize social evils and bring any change in the society. More than the laws, it is the active cooperation and willful participation of various voluntary organisations and constant public vigil which if joined hands with the legal machinery and enforcement machinery will bring tangible results and positive changes. Therefore, the role of voluntary sector may be stressed. Voluntary organizations especially women's organisations have to play a significant role in the battle against dowry with it strategic and fatal implications for women. Already some in metropolitan cities, other cities and major towns are actively involving themselves. They have mobilized public opinion, exerted pressure on the police and an equally apathetic legal system and aged demonstrations. Some of them have been well recognized. Yet, they need to be strengthened and spread to all concerns of the country in order to keep constant vigil and watch on the happenings. This approach may be called as "Social Advocacy" which has been widely used to defend groups of people suffering from systematic injustices Social advocacy is an approach in which the change agent system may be an individual, group or organisations, which acts on behalf of aggrieved groups or individuals in order to redress the injustice by approaching the legitimate authority to bring about change in the particular social systems that are causing or perpetuating the injustice.

Here, the agent or organisation which brings change will provide counseling and rehabilitation services to help individual women, educate people on the issue of dowry with the aim of raising their critical consciousness and collaborate with other organisations and professionals working with women. It campaigns through various publicity media alike talks, discussions, hoardings, pamphlets, news items and articles in the print media. Further the organisation will made strenuous efforts to seek proper fulfillment of responsibility by police and lawyers by approaching them in individual cases of women. Action-oriented pilot studies on the attitudes of the parents towards dowry, the legislation on dowry and the loopholes, will also be undertaken. Above all, the approach of Social Advocacy is tremendous and highly useful in combating the dowry evil. The use of Social Advocacy can make a great dent in the problem of dowry. What is however, to be stressed here in that they need to be further strengthened and spread to all district headquarters and towns. A strong liason has to be maintained between the organisation, police and the legal machinery. The likeminded can come together and form such agents of change at national, state, district and local levels and a close coordination has to be maintained for the successful functioning and building up a strong base for the struggle.

Dowry is Raising the Status of Women

Most of the social problems like dowry have badly affected the status of women in the society. The practice of dowry has been generally accepted as a social custom and a social problem for those who cannot pay dowry. In recent years, it has become more complex. In the process a large number of innocent girls have suffered from, atrocities, humiliation, continued harassment stress and strains. The cases of girls committing suicide and bride-burning are the extreme forms of this social problem. It is not only socio-psychological but also economic in nature. It has also a status symbol and has socio-legal aspects. It may be observed that in the matter of demanding and giving dowry, women themselves play a predominant role. Hence they can play some positive role in counting this social evil.

Education holds the key to the progress of an individual and is the most important instrument for social transformation. It is an indication of women's status. The degree of women's participation in social, economic and political life will largely depend upon her educational status. It is therefore necessary to improve the literacy status of women as this is responsible for their lower status. Though the constitutional provisions and the Five-year plans have contributed to the progress of women's education, there is still a lot to be done in this field. Proper social environment has to be created to bring about qualitative change in Women's education as this will augment women's empowerment in social transformation.

Legal literacy is another area which requires to be promoted among women. This has to be made part of curriculum at the graduate level, as this will create and generate more awareness among girls to deal with complex social situations effectively and boldly. For improving the status of women, girls should be educated and trained to fight against atrocities, harassment and murderous attempts rather than accepting these quietly. They should be given equal opportunities of growth and development education and share in family property. They should be taught dignity of labor and freedom. Factors such as women's education, economic, independence providing equal opportunities, to girls in the families, awareness of laws concerning women and women's organisations can help in improving the status of women. However unless the deep-rooted gender bias is removed from our society, social problems will continue to adversely affect women.

IT appears as thought education instead of mitigating and condemning dowry as a social evil has only perpetuated it as a necessary evil. It is here that education for young women could serve as an instrument for social change. The educated women have an onerous responsibility towards themselves, their families and the society to utilize their education to secure economic independence. Through economic independence, they would establish an identity of their own. The dowry problem calls for a reassessment of social, moral values among the youth, and a reshuffling of priorities among the women in particular. If this is established the women can certainly put an end to dowry.

Dowry is not an individual's problem it is a problem of

concern to all, a social problem which has reached monstrous proportions. It I not a problem of the present or the past; but an age-old custom which has social and religious sanctions. The pernicious dowry in its present form is a product of the patriarchal tradition and the new unequal socio-economic development introduced by the colonialists and the post-colonialist governments. It ugly hydra-headed form is all pervasive, affecting particularly the less-affluent and the poor causes/castes than the more affluent and the rich. It has not only affected the position of women. But miserably degraded their status in the society. It has become one of the major sources of human misery and causes for marital disharmony. It has generated a vicious evil of sociological corruption. Thus it is one of the most difficult and serious challenges to the present day society. Such a complex problem requires an integrated social endeavour to successfully overcome it. It has to e fought on various fronts, legal, social, education, cultural and political. So many legal laws, penal laws etc., are available to check this phenomenon. So many anti-dowry processions to check this phenomenon. So many anti-dowry processions and demonstrations are organized by voluntary groups. But this evil practice continues on unabled. Legal battle against the evil is one: Social movement is another. What is more urgently required is a radical change in human consciousness. Nothing else but a substantial radical change in human psyche alone can bring some change in the society, no matter whether legal actions and social movements are resorted to. All legislation and a all social movements are resorted to. All legislations and all social movements are external to man. These may bring some peripheral changes in the structure. But it is ultimately the individual, the basic unit of he society, who can bring greater changes and this is possible only when a radical, and total metamorphosis takes place in he human psyche.

Some Case Study

The Report on April 14, 1977, Daily News Paper, Indian Express. Prominent citizens met the Assistant Superintendent of Police and the Station House Officer of the Gurgaon police station here today and urged them to expedite investigation into the circumstances of the death of Krishna Kumari (24) on April 12, within two months of her marriage. The father-in-law of Krishna Kumari, a trained teacher, had lodged a report with the police on April 12 that she had committed suicide by setting fie to her clothes. But the post-mortem report said that Krishna Kumari had died of asphyxiation and that the burns seemed to have been caused after she had died of asphyxiation." Following the post-mortem report the police have registered a case of murder.

The father of the girl, who owns a tailoring shop here fears that Krishna Kumari might have been murdered. His fear is based on the knowledge that the girl's in-laws were dissatisfied with the dowry given to her at the time of her marriage.

He told this correspondent as also the police today that Krishna Kumari had often come to him to say that her in laws wanted more dowry. A private medical officer of the town told the police the Krishna Kumari had visited him once to take medicines for insomnia, which she said was caused by the harassment by her in-laws. The headmaster of the school where Krishna Kumari taught till recently said that she had confided in him that she was being ill treated by the in-laws. A sister-in-law of Krishna Kumari alleged that Krishna Kumari's in-laws never informed her parents aunt the alleged suicide. Somehow, she happened to visit the house that very day and learnt of the incident. It was she who informed Krishna Kumari's father of the death, she claimed.

According to her, when he saw Krishna Kumari's body her tongue was bulging out and some blood was also following doctors say this can happen only in the case of asphyxiation and no tin the case of suicide by setting one's clothes on fire. One of the neighbours interrogated by the police said that he had heard shrieks of the girl.

A day before the incident, Krishna Kumari and her husband had returned form a visit to the Vaishno Devi Shrine." The father-in-law of the deceased Krishna Kumari had reported to the police on 12th April, 1977 as follows: Krishna Kumari was married to his eldest son Hira Lal on 10th February, 1977. Hira Lal was working as a Stenographer in the Agriculture Ministry in Delhi where Krishna Kumari was working as teachers in Farukhnagar, district Gurgaon. A couple of days before the incident, Hira Lal and Krisna Kumari had returned from a trip to Vaishno Devi, Jammu. On the day of incident he was informed by his daughter on telephone that Krishna Kumari was in a bad condition. She was declared as dead by Dr. Grover, who had accompanied him to the house.

The police got a post-mortem examination of the body conducted. The doctor opined as follows:

"In my opinion death was probably caused by asphyxiation and the clear sign of the burns strongly suggested that burns are post-mortem in nature."

The police registered a case of murder as suggested by the post-mortem examination report. The father of the deceased sent the following complaints to various authorities:

"Subject: Dowry motived heinous murder of the newly married trained M.A. B.Ed. teacher, daughter of a poor tailor, in the house of her in-laws in Gurgaon.

Sir, I being the unfortunate father of the deceased, approach you with the following facts on the above cited subject for favour of kind personal attention and immediate action:

Telegrams were despatched to the concerned higher Executive and Police authorities on 12-5-77 by me, the poor and unfortunate father of the deceased girl requesting for immediate action and investigation into the crime of murder of my daughter Krishna Kumari aged 24 years and in robust health, an M.A. B.Ed teacher who was married recently with Sh. Hira Lal and who has met her death at the altar of dowry.

Prima facie clinching material is available to connect the accused person with murder of a recently married daughter of mine, a poor tailor in Gurgaon and yet no arrest has been made so far although a case u/s 302 IPC has been registered.

Evidence of the following circumstances connected with the

crime is in existence. The criminals are suspected to have exercised influence to avoid their arrest and to misguide and misdirect investigation. The dirty part played by some persons including a Congress Leader of New Colony, Gurgaon in order to suppress the truth and shield the culprits is well-known in the area. The deceased Krishna Kimari, a healthy bride of 24 years of age, was found dead in the house of her-in-laws, only about two months after the marriage. evidence regarding the deceased having been last seen with the four accused namely her father-in-law Shrin Mulkh Raj Duggal, her husband Sh. Hira Lal, Smt. Rah Rani maternal aunt of her husband who is popularly known to be living with the widower father-in-law of the deceased as his keep and Veena, sister of Sh. Hira Lal is available in abundance. Thousands of residents of the area have affirmed their conviction that the girl has lost her life due to machination of her husband and the in-laws including Smt. Raj Rani.

Clinching and unshakable evidence of greed for valuable dowry by the in-laws exists as the strong motive for the crime. Absence of any gold ornaments such as ear tops, mangal sutra, ring and bangles which the deceased always had on her person and which were found missing on the dead body providing an incriminating clue. Existence of rubber bangles on the wrist of the deceased would lead to the inference that in he display of treachery and foolish ingenuity, the said culprits created material to exculpate themselves of the crime.

The dead body was foundling in a small kitchen of the house of her in-laws in a state of rigor mortals. The wooden chaukis lying about 6' away from the idea body were found without any signs of smoke or burns of fire the kitchen door which was at a distance of a few inches from the body had similarly no signs of fire burns or smoke. The utensil lying in the kitchen were fund in orderly form and quite undisturbed. No carbon or ash resulting from the burnt clothes was found on the utensials or anywhere also in the kitchen. The floor too was uncharred. There was no sign of smoke or burns on the walls or ceiling of the kitchen. There smoke or burns on the walls or ceiling of the kitchen. There were no boils (Chhalas) on any part o the body. All these facts were brought to the notice of the police on the spot at the time of their investigation and preparation of report on 12-4-1977 by the parents and other prominent persons.

Post-mortem examination of the dead body has supplied positive evidence that the girl died of asphyxia and that the burns present on the dead body were caused after her death and are not ante-mortem. This destroys the wicked and invented story that the deceased died due to shock from suicidal burns.

No smell of kerosene oil was found in the kitchen by any of the witnesses who saw the dead body immediately after Smt. Santosh's visit to her in laws' house on 12-4-1977. No independent eye witness saw her committing suicide as is alleged. All evidence thus leads to the only conclusion that after her murder, her dead body was placed in the kitchen and the burns were caused by the culprits to the dead body to prove there concocted story of suicide.

The husband of the deceased was not present soon after the murder. The father-in-law of the deceased and her husband never informed her parents or any member of her parent's family of the argue some tragedy till I learnt about it on the chance visit to the house of Shri Hira Lal by my daughter-in-law Smt. Santosh to invite the newly married couple and her in-laws for a dinner on Baisakhi festival i.e. 13-4-1977 being the first Baisakhi after marriage.

To prove the motive the prosecution relief upon the evidence of Santosh Kumari (P.W. 14), who is the sister-in-law of the deceased Saroj (P.W. 16), sister of the deceased, Mohan Lal (P.W. 15), Madan Lal Kapoor (P.W. 17), Onkar Kapoor (P.W. 22) Saroj Chopra (P.W. 26) and Wasanda Rani (P.W. 23), father of the deceased. The version of Wasanda Ram (P.W. 23), is that when he went for the Shaggan ceremony in the company of Joginder Singh and Gopal Das PWs, the accused-respondents re-acted as to what had been brought in the dowry and why Frig. And TV had not been brought, whereupon he promised that he would supply these articles gradually. The aforesaid remaining witnesses have corroborated the version of Wasanda Ram (P.W. 23). This evidence provides a strong motive for the respondents to have committed this crime. The deceased was an educated lady, who was not suffering from any ailment. She had no cause to end her life by committing suicide. She was an earning hand. She could leave her husband. Moreover, when the educated ladies commit suicide they generally leave a written note behind so that no innocent person may be involved. Krishna Kumari had also served breakfast to her husband on the date of occurrence in the morning.She had also accompanied her husband to Vaishno devi and had come back rom they two days before the occurrence. The aforesaid witness Hve no animus against the respondence. As most of them are residents of gurgaonand are of the same brotherhood. Their testimony amply proves that the respondents were pressing for television and refrigiratorand were harassing krishna kumari deceased.

CHAPTER 3

Causes and Factors of Divorce

An attempt is made in he following pages to examine the causes of divorce and its effects in preventive and remedial measures are suggested to make divorce a socially useful instrument. Divorce which had existed in one form or the other since the pre-historic period has been legally sanctioned under every system of law all over the world, but in the actual working of the legal system the divorced women and children have not received adequate legal protection. In India while divorce has the religious and legal sanction it has adversely affected the lives of women and children. The legal aspects related to divorce are discussed elsewhere in the section of "Women, law and social Change."

Causes of Divorce

The legal bases for divorce and the actual conditions leading to divorce need not be the same and very often they are different. What the law provides as grounds for divorce are the legally sustainable grounds, for divorce are the legally sustainable grounds, largely drawn from the religious injunctions. But in actual practice, divorce, legally valid or otherwise, is caused by a host of socio-economic, religious and psychological factors affecting the inter-spousal relationship. There are several factors that affect the divorce decision, such as the a great marriage, child birth, income, education of the souses, their immediate family environment, the religious or cultural perception of the individuals and the health status of the spouses. Identification of the real causes of divorce is attempted wit a view to understand the conditions under which individuals are more likely to terminate their marriage instead of continuing it.

The environmental factors in turn can be sub-divided into: (i) endogenous factors and (ii) exogenous factors. The endogenous environmental factors are those that affect the socio-economic and cultural status of the family and the individual's reactions to these factors. These factors also include the intra-familiar issues such as parental disharmony or parent-child relationship.

The important environmental factors exogenous to the family are income, family size, family assets, health status of its members, age indisparity between the spouses, the age at marriage and the like. Dowry and the spouse's working career also affect the marital stability and lead to divorce. The personality factors affecting divorce include the nature of the spouses, their perceptions, values, adjustment and mental development, Impotency barrenness and illicit relations are the other important individual specific factors affecting manual relationship and contributing to divorce.

In the early sociological studies done by Damre, Kuppuswamy; Fonseca and others, the investigators argue that the real causes of divorce as different from legal causes are childlessness, failure to fulfill the obligations of marriage, unhappy married life, domestic disharmony, infidelity, poverty, poor living conditions, low education, poor health, and age gap between the spouses.

Legal causes of divorce do not necessarily reflect the reality of the marital conflicts. The legal system often requires the 'innocent' party to prove that the other is guilty in marital behaviour. By the time the suit is filed, both the parties would have agreed to obtain a divorce and they simply utilize the grounds that are legally most effective and socially least damaging to both. Following the standard, four-fold classifications, the main causes of divorce are presented as follows:

Biological Factors: Sexual relationship between the souses is one of the important aspects of marital adjustment. The sexual relationship between the spouses gets severely affected if either or both the spouses indulge in illicit sexual relationship, is if either of the spouse is impotent or imbecile. When couples do not conform to the socially and culturally accepted norms of sexual conduct, is proved or discovered if may lead to divorce. Illicit relations as the cause of strained marital relations and divorce has been reported as the principal cause of divorce in India but all illicit relationships even when discovered do not lead to divorce due to family and social control over the spouses. It all depends on the socio-economic position of he spouses and their adjustment. In any case, the discovery of illicit relationship on the part of either spouses, invariably places the women in a more vulnerable position than the men. The society treats the man and the women differently even when both are proved to have had illicit relations.

Though no longer a legal ground barrenness is reported as an important factor responsible for dissolution of marriage and divorce in India. Indians in general and the Hindus in particular do not accept childlessness with resignation. A barren women does to enjoy the sacramental rights in social life. It is not uncommon to blame the women even when the husband's sterility is responsible for the barrenness. In India, men getting remarried on the assumption that the first wife is barren is not uncommon. Several studies have reported that the first wives, even when they were not really sterile, suffer silently rather than preferring divorce. Thus, illicit relations impotency and barrenness, whether proved or not have strained relations, affecting the interests of women.

Social Factors

Several social factors strain marriage and lead to divorce. Differences in the family background and status of the spouses, family structure, immaturity at marriage and age disparity between the spouses are often reported to have strained marital relationship. An important source of conflict for the partners is the multiple roles they are expected to perform in the modern context. This is particularly true of a women, who has to perform the role of a wife, a mother, a companion and sometimes the head of the household simultaneously. Very often the roles of a women do not fit into the joint family structure. This results in conflict. Further even the husband in such a family may resists the assumption of authority by a woman, contributing to marital instability. The role conflict problems are particularly noticeable when the wife is employed. The economic role played by an employed women in a family is often resisted by the husband and his parents. The conflict is more serious when both the spouses are not employed in the same place and when the wife is called upon to shoulder greater responsibilities.

There is another factor that contributes to strained relations between the wife and the husband. Some husbands physically assault their wives on flimsy grounds, often on the complaints of other members of the family. Eh wife is beaten on trivial matters such as waking up lat, being lazy and lethargic, for inefficient cooking and for reprimanding children; When the marriage is already under stress, such physical assaults only lead to family discord, disharmony and sometimes to divorce. The women is the victim in all such cases.

Quite often, the matchmakers suppress some information relating to physical deformities defects of the girl/boy at the time of match making. After the marriage, when the deformities or defects are discovered or known, or interfere with the normal functioning, the marital relationship reaches a breaking pint. In most of such cases, the women becomes the unfortunate victim.

Happy marital life presupposes certain minimum living, conditions such as decent accommodation, privacy and at home entertainment. When decent living conditions do not exist, the spouses will be forced to live a stressful life leading to discord and family disharmony. Absence of decent living conditions effect the women much more than the man. For example cramped living rooms, inconvenient kitchen, ill-equipped bathrooms, and inadequate water supply, affect the women in her daily life much more than the husband. Poor living conditions in joint families render the woman's life more miserable.

Very wide age gap between the spouses is not desirable for a happy marriage as, such a gap, creates problems of emotional adjustment and understanding.

Economic Factors

Several economic factors such as the income, asset and employment status of the husband, the amount and forms of dowry and working status of the wife, influence the success of a marriage. When the husband is poor with low income and has no valuable property, he may fail to support the family adequately resulting in the economic hardship to the family which may eventually lead to the break-up of marriage. Secondly, when the amount and form of dowry promised is not given entirely and in he agreed form, it is bound to result in strained relations and in quite a few cases divorce as well. In many such cases, the husband's parents and other family members harass the wife and aggravate intra-family tensions. The plight of the less educated and unemployed women suffering on account of dowry related problems is pitiable.

Psychological Factors

A spouse's attitude towards the partner depends among other things on the personality traits. The personality traits are dependent to a large degree on the psychological aspects of the individual such as the attitude to work, ability to maintain calm in times of emergency, the general temperament (pleasant or irritable), and the nature of the person (domineering, equal or subservient) The psychological aspects mould the temperament of the individual and his or her emotional reactions. The temperamental qualities are in turn determined by the qualities of the individual. These qualities can e subdued but cannot be eliminated. Couples who are given to such temperamental traits and sensitivity are prone to abnormal reactions even for small matters. Similarly, when one of the spouses has a domineering nature he or she tries to dominate over the other person and influence his or her decisions. When the other person resists, it results in family strife. Marriage essentially requires accommodation, integration, and certain amount of sacrifice on the part of both the spouses. When one person is domineering, then it would result in conflict between the two. When ego is involved, the domineering nature of one person may have serious consequences to the marriage. In a traditional family, the physical husband and wife relationship is marked by male dominance and female sub service and dependence. But when the actual spousal relationship is different from the mutually expected relationship, then the differences surface, sometimes resulting in the dissolution of marriage. Much depends on various concomitant factors-social, economic and biological. Women on the average appear to have suffered more on account of the psychological factors. Generally husbands from urban tend to be more dominant than those form rural areas. The wives from rural areas however, tacitly accept such dominance.

Many empirical studies have reported that problems of maladjustment between the spouses is more pronounced in the "upper castes", while in the "lower castes" the adjustment problems are fewer. But the social and biological factors are as important in creating conflicts between the spouses, in lower and intermediate castes as in upper caste. In the Indian family setting, the daughter-in-law's relationship with parents-in-law also influences, the relationship between the spouses. Between the parents-in-law, eh mother-in-law is reported to have a stronger influence over the inter-spousal relationship.

According to Gary Becker, who sees family as a joint enterprise run by both the spouses, sharing of work and social activities, is essential for successful running of the family enterprise. In the opinion of Goode, the relationship between husband and wife suffers when the spouses do not share family activities along the expected lines such as cooking, gardening, entertainment, social visits and economic activities. While divorce is a product of a complex web of socio-economic, biological and cultural factors, the relative importance of each set of factors varies from one case to another. Ore importantly depending on the nature and severity of the causes, marriages break down sooner or later. Large number of studies have reported that biological factors. Such as impotency and illicit relations result in early divorce. Social factors, such as, authority and role conflicts and physical assaults lead to divorce relatively slowly.

Divorce is considered by the proponents of feminism as an instrument which can free women from unwanted incompatible marriage. But the marriage does not involve women alone or the marriage alone. As far as the divorce between a man and women, who have no children is concerned, the above argument could be accepted, of course, with reservations. Even in the case, where the couple do not have children, the woman will be free, provided she is economically independent. The instrument of divorce is often used by the males to get rid off 'old wife' to array a new one. As far as the Indian Penal Code is concerned there not limit for the number of 'legal' marriages a person can enter into.

Effects of Divorce

Emotional Problems: Divorce is the end of a marriage. But for the divorce couples, it marks the beginning of several for the divorced couples, it mars the beginning of several problem. The first problem that confronts the divorced couple is the emotional adjustment. The separated persons have to reckon with the new realities. The husband has to adjust in his emotional life, personal habits business and social life. The wife has to make all these adjustments and in addition she had to seek socio-economic support. If there are children, their care adds a new dimension to both the parties. Persons with strong well integrated life may survive divorce with ease. But people with less integrated personalities may find it difficult to reconcile and adjust to the post-divorce realities.

Given the social conditions in India, for most women, divorce is like jumping from the frying pan into the fire. It is difficult for the woman to avoid the post divorce realities. Sometimes, she has to control the conflict and rebellion within herself. She has to learn to live without a companion or with a new companion. She has to cultivate a new relationship with the children. She has to reorient her sexual life. The husband also faces most of these problems after divorce.

Economic Effects: The process of economic adjustment for women after divorce is the most difficult one. The women divorce may secure alimony or seek a job. She may rely upon her property or live on her parent's property, if any. Living on alimony] is generally disliked by women. Seeking employment after divorce is a better course but findings a secure and honorable ob is not easy. For the uneducated woman, the consequences are too serious to withstand, Sometimes women have to face humiliation in the process of seeking economic support.

A women with children to care for may find it all the more difficult to adjust after the divorce. Sometimes, the divorced woman may not receive acceptance or support from her parents. Very often the ex-husbands fail to pay alimony resulting in economic distress to the women and children. Several studies have reported that the divorce, adversely affects the consumption pattern, saving capacity and the economic status of the women and children. To some extent, the adverse economic effects of divorce are found in respect of the husband too. The sense of economic security that is associated with the marriage will be absent, after the divorce even if spouses have some assured income and property.

Marriage After Divorce: Once the marriage is dissolved the divorced are free to choose new partners if they desire. Several studies in India show that a good majority of the males below 45 years of age marry a new spouse after divorce. However, for the woman the incidence of marriage after divorce is very low especially if she has children from the first marriage. Both the spouses may have emotional and adjustment problems in the remarriage.

Children of the Divorced: Children need parental love, affection and security. When divorce occurs the children may not be aware of the reasons behind their parents divorce. But they suffer its consequences. In all cases of divorce, the custody of the children is a major problem. In the majority of the cases custody is given to the mother. The children under the care of either the mother or the father have to live an incomplete family life. Sometimes, they may be torn between the divorced parents. Left to the father's care, they cannot get the mother's care, affection and love. The children raised under such family circumstances may develop several emotional and adjustment problems, which can have an adverse impact in their lives.

Triple Talaq Controversy: Several muslim women's organizations had appealed to the All India Muslim Law Board to declare the triple talaq as antis islamic. According to one opinion the Holy Quran does not approve of divorce by triple talaq. It is said that the Quran required appointment of two arbiters, one by the women and the other by the man for taking decision regarding the divorce. In May 1993 a body of Muslim theologians issued a fatwa in a case referred to them invalidating the triple talaq given at one sitting, whereby, a muslim husband could unilaterally divorce his wife without assigning any reasons. Within a week of this event, the Jammat-Ulemas-Hind, a central body of Sunni Theologians published a statement upholding the validity of the triple talaq. The Muslim society in India practices divorce largely through triple talaz despite the holy Quran not approving divorce by triple talaq.

There are many apprehensions and misinterpretations of the personal Jaws relating to divorce; and remarriages. Recently a body of religious heads. of the muslim community, in incident of uttering talaq thrice for getting divorce, has remarked That It was a sort of mockery of the orders of holy Qurn. Talaq should be uttred once as the first warning to the woman and before witnesses. After a lapse of one month if the situation does not improve second talaq to be uttered in front of witnesses. Finally in the third month if the word talaq is utterd again in front of witnesses only then the divorce comes into force. In all the three instances this ritual should be performed only after the woman has her regular menstruation. This procedure is known only to very few person even within the muslim community. A woman is also at liberty for Khula, that is divorce from the man if there is dispute between the couple. For this also, se has to call a meeting of relatives as well as local priests for guidance and to witness. Analysing both the pros and cons of a divorce one can come to the conclusion that divorce is an instrument which should be used as a last resort when all other means to ensure the success of a marriage fail.

Besides the aforementioned legal battle, social advocacy approach, and other effective steps, some more steps may be taken up in order to contain this most dreaded social evil. The following are the same suggestions and recommendations in this regard which may help ameliorate the situation.

The Anti-Dowry Cells which are functioning in some main metropolitan cities of the country should be created in all major towns and district head quarters. And all these should be interlinked at state and national levels for better coordination and effective functioning To strengthen these cells, they should be given more powers in terms of taking actions.

Topic of divorce and its various manifestations, its effects on the family, on the spouse etc, are to be part of the curriculum for learning preferably at: the under graduate level, Both boys and girls should be exposed to this instruction at a suitable level in their educational programme.

People in general should be made aware and educated on divorce and its effects on the family members through powerful audio visual media such as the T.V. or the street plays.

It should be made mandatory for the advocates to refer the divorce petitioners to a marriage counselor first before filing the divorce petition. The counselling should focus on the adverse effects of separation, to both the spouses and their children. A Femina Survey of couples with problems revealed that 72 per cent of the respondents had constant discussions and they tried their best at reconciliation. The survey also revealed that in 53 per cent of cases parents helped reconciliation, in 38 per cent friends helped and in 29 percent the in laws tried to help. Only ten per cent of respondents went to marriage-counsellors, 3 per cent sought medical help and, another 3 per cent went to religious heads of priests but in cases where the marriage ultimately failed, many of these efforts did not have a positive impact.

Awareness therefore is very important not only regarding the laws of divorce but the ways in which they should be applied when the situation arises.

Even in extreme cases where divorce is a must, the children should be put under the care of the parents in such a way that their overall well being is not neglected.

Counseling plays a great role when divorce is inevitable. This has a special role in trying to help children of divorced parents who suffer internal fears in their mind when the parents walk away leaving the children to themselves or under the institutional care. Some children become sick physically, mentally and some children take to drugs, alcohol, and other self abuses.

CHAPTER 4

Relevant Response of International Labour Organisation for Trafficking of Girls and Children

The ILO report concludes with a series of proposals to fight forced labour. For a start it, it recommends tackling the roots of the problem, which arise from causes such as discrimination, deprivation and poverty. Then it calls for remedying defects such as inadequate regulation and weak and non-existent labour inspections. It also urges the adoption of clear legislation and the delegation of real power to law enforcement agents. The report also urges countries to put in place comprehensive rehabilitation programmes to support the victims of forced labour.

It is an accepted fact that, even on the threshold of the 21st century, there is no section of our society Chore oppressed, more exploited and more neglected than women. In every segment, class or community, women suffer the consequences of gender discrimination too. Yet, their contribution in economic life, social well-being, cultural continuity and ethical standards is far greater than their share of the population. A national daily of Delhi commented on 29th January, 1995 under the caption 'Cries of Oppression' that, "While we progress technologically, earning ourselves a reputation for a world of satellites, missiles and fifth generation computers, we have also acquired the distinction of recording one rape in every 42 minutes, besides increased cases of crimes against women, including molestation, stripping, eve-teasing, kidnapping, dowry deaths female foeticide, even sati, and the lakhs of women who are abused and battered by their husbands in the privacy of their own homes.

The International Labour Organisation (ILO) Report

The International Labour Organisation (ILO) discussed a report entitled, *Global Alliance against Forced Labour*. ILO Director- General, Juan Somavia called a such labour, "A social evil which has no place in modern world". He added, "To achieve a fair globalisation and decent work for all, it is imperative to eradicate forced labour."

The report starts by defining *the concept of forced labour*. It is not to be confused with poor working conditions or sub-standard wages. Rather, ILO considers *two elements* are involved in forced labour: *the work or service is exacted under the menace of a penalty; and it undertaken involuntarily.*

The report estimates that 12.3 million people are trapped in forced labour. This figure is a "minimum estimate" that probably errors on the low side, the study acknowledgements. Most of the people affected by this phenomenon are in Asia, with some 9.5 million forced labourer. Latin America and the Caribbean follow with 1.3 million. Of the 12.3 million forced labourer, 9.8 million are exploited in the private sector. Another 2.5 million are forced to work by Governments like in China or by Rebel Military Groups.

The forms of forced labour are vary widely. In the past slavery or bonded labour was common and still persists in many countries, particularly in Asia. More modern forms are often linked to migratory labour and trafficking in persons for commercial reasons, often involving women and children in activities ranging from drug dealing to begging to sexual exploitation. Migrant workers in many places are often obliged to hand-over identity documents and find themselves tied to one household with restricted freedom of movement.

The report calculates that at least 2.4 million people are victims of human trafficking. The report estimates that the profits generated by the exploitation of trafficked women, children and men are in the region of $32 billion a year or about $13,000 per victim.

A breakdown of the data shows regional differences in the composition of the type of forced labour. In Asia, Latin America and sub-Saharan Africa the proportion of trafficked victims is under 20 per cent of all forced labour. In industrialised countries in labour transition countries and in the Middle East and north African countries, however, trafficking accounts for more than 75 per cent of forced labour. The report notes that in practice there is frequently a mixture of human smuggling and trafficking.

Many of those who end up in forced labour have migrated voluntarily and become victims on their way to or at their destination. The main types of work affected by trafficking are the sex industry, agriculture, domestic work and construction. It also occurs in the sector of restaurants and catering, as well as in small sweatshop enterprises.

Causes of Forced Labour and Trafficking

The report observes there is no unanimity over what causes forced labour. In developing countries, the overwhelming majority of victims of forced labour are poor. In many cases, the demand is linked to a pattern of discrimination according to caste, class and gender. There is an ongoing debate whether the lack of rural credit and markets, agrarian ownership patterns and unequal power relationships explain the persistence of forced labour. Nor is it clear, the report states, to what extent the current trend of globalisation contributes to new forms of forced labour.

Towards a Relevant Response

One of the serious difficulties that impede efforts at addressing the issue trafficking is that the definitions of trafficking and forced labour are so general that it is difficult to prove in court in practice. The ILO report concludes with a series of proposals to fight forced labour. For a start it, it recommends tackling the roots of the problem, which arise from causes such as discrimination, deprivation and poverty. Then it calls for remedying defects such as inadequate regulation and weak and non-existent labour inspections. It also urges the adoption of clear legislation and the delegation of real power to law enforcement agents. The report also urges countries to put in place comprehensive rehabilitation programmes to support the victims of forced labour.

The Vatican Conference on Human Trafficking

In RCME, on June 30, 2005 participants at a Vatican Conference on the world's growing sex trade concluded that the time has arrived for the Church to take bigger steps toward freeing modern day slaves. Officials said that *human trafficking is the third biggest crime in the world, rivaling the illicit sale of drugs and arms*. Archbishop Marchetto insisted that it's not good enough for us to just sit back and watch while the "saints" do the work.

An estimated 500,000 women from Eastern Europe are enslaved and forced to prostitute themselves on the streets of Western Europe alone. The data are even more staggering from Asia, India, Africa and the Americas. Catholic organisations and religious communities are already active in the field of rescuing the victims of human trafficking.

Yet, Archbishop Agostino Marchetto, the secretary of the host Pontifical Council, indicated how the Church could improve in its role, especially in raising public awareness of the scourge. "I believe that it's a problem and Phenomenon affecting each country, and because the universal church is incarnated in the different local Churches, it is important that every single one should have a conscious awareness of it."

Archbishop Marchetto said, "They should aim at giving visibility to this problem. In spite of it being known, its intricacies are highly unknown." He translated this to mean that *bishops will have to place trafficking on their agendas*. "I hope that from here, the various bishops' conferences may realise how vital this battle is."

An Article "A Cargo of Exploitable Souls" (May 30th 2002)

It reveals that America, a "prime tourist destination", is also a prime destination for much less happy people. One group, impoverished young girls from Mexico, was found earlier this year in a suburban house in New Jersey. They had been lured from their home towns by an international trafficking rings, smuggled to the United States and forced into prostitution. The victims, who were beaten if they resisted, sold their bodies to customers for as little as $35.

The article points out that *trafficking is defined as forcing people to migrate from one place to the other through process of allurement or ear.* Mostly the word trafficking is used in the context of prostitution, which is a very narrow definition. *There I trafficking of children, domestic workers, and men workers taking place all the time. Trafficking is distinguished from mere immigrant-smuggling by the degree of coercion, deception and exploitation.*

Every year, on State Department estimates, about 50,000 people, the vast majority women and children, are forcibly trafficked into the United States from all over the world—Eastern Europe, Asia, Central America, Africa. Once there, most victims disappear among the 8 million or so other illegal immigrants in the country. They are forced to work as virtual slaves. For the traffickers' profit, in the sex industry, on arms and in factories. The victims, who rarely speak English, exist in a sort of parallel universe with no money, no documents, the threat of beatings and limited contact with anyone but their keepers and other victims.

Since the passage in 2000 of the Trafficking Victim Protection Act, pioneering by Congressman Chris Smith, both investigations and prosecutions have been stepped up. The Department of Justice had 111 investigations of human trafficking opening mid-May, a 50 per cent increase over the year before. In fiscal 2001 the department prosecuted 34 traffickers, four times as many as a year earlier. Those convicted of trafficking may now receive up to 20 years in prison and, in some cases, life sentences.

America's Anti-trafficking Efforts Extend Overseas

The State Department's first annual human-trafficking report, issued in June 2005, was especially critical of 23 countries—among them Israel, Greece, South Korea, Russia and Pakistan. They, in turn, were upset at being singled out, but Mr Smith is delighted. "We got a lot of backlash, but I am glad they're upset," he says "Friends don't let friends commit human-rights abuses."

An estimated 400,000 children are victims of prostitution and other forms of commercial sex in the United States. The vast majority of them are Americans, including many blue-eyed blondes from the mid-west.

The Trafficking Trap

The US named four Gulf allies as among the worst at combating human trafficking. Thousands of men, women, and children, most of them from Asia, will be trafficked to the Gulf to live as what the us State Department calls "modern day slaves." Most won't know until they get here what lies in store for them and hundreds will flee their employers, suffer physical, emotional and/or sexual abuse, and go home empty-handed.

In June 2003 the US State Department listed Kuwait, Qatar, Saudi Arabia, and the United Arab Emirates (UAE) among 14 countries that do little or nothing to stop human trafficking. Washington lowered all four to its Tier 3 category, which could eventually lead to economic sanctions if these countries do not act to stem the flow of trafficking across their borders.

The State Department says that 600,000 to 800,000 men, women, and children worldwide are victims of trafficking—the recruitment, transportation, or harboring of people by means of threat, force, coercion, fraud, or deception for the purpose of exploitation and forced labour.

There are no raw numbers on how many of these trafficked persons—who can end up being maids, factory workers, camel jockeys, or prostitutes—come to the Middle East. But the Gulf boasts one of the highest populations of expatriate labour forces in the world, with more than 10 million. In Kuwait, there is an average of one maid for every two Kuwaitis and in the UAE, 1.6

million people, or 80 per cent of the total population, are expatriate workers.

The thousands of Bangladeshi, Filipino, Indonesian, Sri Lankan, and other Asian women and men who seek sanctuary at their embassies across the region each week see little improvement in their conditions. As most locals will acknowledge, the lifestyle of Gulfies (nationals from any of the Arab Gulf states) is built on a foundation of foreign labour. Most citizens' households – including high-ranking government officials, human rights advocates, as well as labour activities—have at least one and often several servants including a driver, cook, and maid.

Recruiting scams are all too common. Trafficking victims say nationals from their home countries, as well as embassy official and local citizens, often conspire to "recruit" hundreds of labourers, in exchange for a fee. Too often, such recruits find themselves homeless, jobless, and seeking sanctuary in their embassies or being arrested and deported.

The Fight Against Trafficking

In the trafficking report, the US outlines specifically what measures it expects countries identified as the worst offenders to undertake in order to improve the situation. James Miller, senior adviser to the secretary of State and director of the Office to Monitor and Combat Trafficking in Persons, called on the government to combat its problems with "modern day slavery" by raising public awareness, improving labour laws to protest victims, and prosecuting offenders.

Some young women who are trapped into domestic servitude and often abused, see no way out of their situation other than suicide. Instances of young Asian maids killing themselves by hanging or jumping off high buildings are a regular occurrence. Therefore, the simple logic is that there is an increasing demand in society for sex and cheap labour. Secondly, there is always a source base from where the supply is met. *One of the best ways of combating trafficking* is, *therefore, to prevent it from source area.*

Dealing with Trafficking in India

The National Human Rights Commission (NHRC) study (Times of India, January 11,2006) highlighted that among the trafficked girls, 20.7 per cent were below 18 years and a majority were pushed into the trade at a very young age. More than 60 per cent of the victims of commercial sexual exploitation were also victims of child marriage. Of them 32.5per cent had been pushed into brothels while they were less than 16 years, while 21.4 per cent where in the 16-17 years age group.

Shockingly, the data shows that 50 per cent of the traffickers were women. While the traffickers adopted different modus operandi. 51.9 per cent lured the victims with job offers and 16.3 per cent with false promises of marriage. Almost 50 per cent of traffickers focused on rural areas for recruitment.

The failure of government in rehabilitation is reflected in the high re-trafficking rate. The study found that 17.5 per cent had been rescued once earlier; 1.8 per cent rescued twice before and 6.6 per cent rescued more than twice. It was also found that more than 57.5 per cent had been arrested earlier. Without proper rehabilitation, it was observed, they have no option but to return to the brothels.

The failure to arrest exploitation in brothels is highlighted by the fact that 34.5 per cent of the brothel owners have never faced any police action during the preceding and 54.4 per cent of them had avoided arrest by bribing police officials.

The study based on interviews with more than 4000 persons demonstrates that more often than not, the victims are the ones who are convicted and fined. Under the existing judicial system, the prosecution has to prove the case against the offender beyond reasonable doubt. This puts a lot of pressure on the victim to convincingly present her case.

What are the Existing Laws in India Dealing with Traffickers?

The first comprehensive legislation to tackle this problem is the Immoral Traffic Prevention Act (ITPA), 1987. The title, immoral traffic itself gives special connotation to sexual morality. Otherwise no need for immoral, since trafficking itself is an immoral act. Hence, the definition of trafficking is extremely important. It should not give thrust to the purpose but to the violence, coercion and deception involved in it.

The objective of the Act are two fold: on the one hand, it wants to check sexual exploitation and abuse of women and children by prescribing heavy punishment to offenders. On the other hand, it seeks to rescue victims of flesh-trade and those in moral danger by providing for a rescue and rehabilitative machinery.

ITPA and Enforcement Agency

* Every offence under IPTA is a cognisable offence. It means the investigating officer can arrest the accused without a warrant (Section 14).
* The special police officer dealing with offences under ITPA should not be below the rank of an Inspector of Police
* The investigating agency (police) has to strictly follow the provisions of Section 13, sub-clause (1) and (2) of ITPA and government notification.
* When writing the First Information Report (FIR) insert Section 4 and connect the offenders of ITPA to the crimes alleged to be committed by them.
* In a police raid, the male customers who visit sex workers in lieu of money should be made prosecution witnesses and not accused persons, as they are the best possible strong eyewitnesses to such incidents.
* Often the accused persons (female sex workers) abscond. Then the police force becomes helpless in executing the warrant of arrest. The investigating officer must frame the prosecution case in most efficient and believable manner and convince the judiciary so as to bring the crime and criminal justice. The burden of proving the case lies on the prosecution.

Shortcomings/Limitations

Despite the amendments, the legislation falls short of objectives and not proved to be very effective measures to check the commercialised flesh trade. The issue is rooted in human nature and the social in equalities: the low status of women and rampant poverty have contributed considerably to such social aberration among women. Without striking at the root cause of the problem, the legislation can only aim at suppression and not prevention.

International Instruments Upholding the Rights of the Trafficked Persons

- The UN Convention for the Suppression of the Traffic in persons and of the exploitation of Prostitution of Others, 1949.
- The Convention on the Elimination of all forms of Discrimination Against Women (CEDAW), 1979.
- The UN Convention on the Rights of the Child (CRC), 1989.
- The Vienna Declaration of 1993 at the World Conference of Human Rights.
- The Beijing Declaration and Platform for Action 1995.
- The ILO Convention on the Worst Forms of Child Labour of 1999.

Constitutional Provisions

* The Government of India ratified an International Convention for the Suppression of Immoral Traffic in Persons and the exploitation of the Prostitution in 1950. Our Constitution upholds the principles of humanism, social and economic justice and the dignity of the individual other with equal protection of law for all its citizens. Victims of prostitution can by no means be debarred from these constitutional rights.
* Article 21 guarantees right to life, which has been interpreted by the Supreme Court in Sunil Batra's case and Bandhua Mukti Morcha case as right to live with dignity.

Article 23 prohibits trafficking in Human beings and any contravention and prohibition is an offence punishable by law. Article 39(I) directs that "health and strength of women and tender age of children shall not be abused and citizens shall not be forced by economic necessity to enter into avocations unsuited to their age or strength."

* Article 41 obligates the state to make effective provisions for securing the right to work and education. Article 51 A makes it a duty upon every citizen and "a fortiori" on the states itself, to eliminate practices derogatory to the dignity of women to develop humanism and practice compassion. Our Constitution thus guarantees right to live with dignity on one hand and exhorts the State to protect women and children from exploitation.

Goa State Consultation on "trafficking in Women and Children" Dec. 17-18, 2005.

The Consultation intended to *create an aware and alert* 'mind' among people in our society, that the phenomena of Trafficking in Women and Children is very much alive in Goa. It aimed (i) to identify the culprits, (ii) to expose their mechanisms of operation (iii) to launch a Campaign to eradicate this crime. Only through a concerted and integrated response form all the sectors of civil society can an adequate response be provided to this heinous crime.

According to the UN Commission on Human Rights (29th February, 2000) definition, *"Trafficking in persons means the recruitment, transportation, purchase, sale transfer, harboring or receipt of a person (i) by threat or use of violence, abduction, force, fraud deception or coercion (including the abuse of authority) or debt bandage for the purpose of and (ii) placing or holding such a person, whether for pay or not, in forced labour or slavery of like practices, in a community other than the one in which such person lived at the time of the original act described in (i)".*

While those who migrate to meet economic needs and those smuggled or trafficked have many vulnerabilities in common, there are important differences between migration and human trafficking. Migration is basically voluntary, while trafficking is forced. The link between migration, human rights and trafficking has gradually been discovered and broader forms of trafficking have been recognised and analysed (debt bondage, slavery, sexual or labour exploitation.)

The Phenomena of Trafficking in Goa

The UN definition is comprehensive, but for Goa we need to more specific. Two aspects of trafficking need to be highlighted: (i) deception and (ii) coercion.

The case studies (see Appendix) and the research presentations at the Consultation highlighted that trafficking in women and children in Goa, like the rest of India and the world, is practiced in many more areas than sexual exploitation of women and children. It is fairly widespread in domestic work, It is concealed in prawn peeling and fish processing units, in stone quarries and among construction labour, in begging for alms, in hotels and small workshops. Only an alert and aware society can discover its hideous forms in hitherto to unknown areas of forced labour involving women and children.

The Role of National and State Policies in Creating both Supply and Demand

Macro-development policies in fact often leave women in debt and unemployed. They migrate in order to live and to help their families/communities. Efforts to tackle trafficking must not overlook the desire of women to migrate in order to improve their own lives and those of their families and children.

The anticipated building boom from the Town and Country Planning Ordinance 2005 will draw an influx of migrant workers and their families from neighbouring States making the women and children vulnerable to trafficking.

The presentation of Goa as a tourism destination for 'sun, sand and sex,' only increases the demand for the sex trade. The ban on bar girls in Mumbai has led to an Influx of them into Goa. The porous borders between India and Bangladesh have encour- d trafficking between the countries extending up to Goa.

Towards a Concerted and Integrated Response

Civil Society is a dynamic concept that networks different institutions, associations and groups in society from the level of families, Mahila Mandals, panchayats right up to political parties, religious institutions and social organisations into collective action for the common good.

The *Consultation* was to sensitise the participants who represent different sectors of society to the horrible experience of those who are trafficked. The *Campaign* that will be launched sometime after this Consultation, will seek the participation of more and more sectors of our society to identify, prevent and prosecute the perpetrators, while rescuing and rehabilitating the victims.

The Consultation indicated *two complementary approaches* to the issue: (i) the *legal approach* of more effective prosecution of the perpetrators (ii) the *cultural approach* that emphasised the need educate civil society to nurture respect for the sacredness and dignity of the victims as persons.

It identified the need to constitute and co-ordinate four working groups:

The success of a Campaign of this nature depends very much upon the quality, accessibility and effective organisation of the material disseminated. Thus, the framework for analyzing the problem of Trafficking in Women and Children will be further sharpened.

Priority will be given to the following research areas where women and children are being traffic, (i) for the flesh trade, (ii) for domestic work, (iii) prawn peeling and fish cleaning industry, (iv) cashew not peeling industry (v) begging, and (vi) any others.

2. *A Legal Aid working Group* that studies how the laws can be more effectively implemented, the police mobilized and the perpetrators prosecuted.

The effectiveness of pertinent laws – States, National, International level – relating to trafficking and child labour and their implementation, even to the extent of involving the Indian Center for Human Rights and Law, the CID and Interpol, will be investigated.

An Education and Advocacy Working Group that will liaise with different sectors of society at State, National and International level to nurture the image of the sacredness and dignity of women and children as the basis of their human rights.

State level demands the mobilisation of different sectors of civil society like the travel and tourism sector, the industrial sector, the builders sector, the academia and other such sectors of civil society as well as the political institutions from panchayat level to State government level.

National Level means networking with national level NGOs and Associations of persons from other States in Goa, particularly those States from where the women and children are trafficked.

International level means involvement with groups like the Asian Human Rights Commission, International Anti Slavery.

4. **A Rescue and Rehabilitation Working Group** that oversees the rescue and rehabilitation services needed by the victims and their repatriation to their own homes.

Conclusion

The *primary focus* in addressing the issue of trafficking should be on targeting the trafficker rather than on harassing the victims.

Secondly the focus should be on the *supply side* (where those trafficked come from and why and the *demand side* (who and what constitutes the reasons for girls and children to be trafficked).

Thirdly, what are the mechanisms used, on the one hand to deceive the victims, on the other hand, to coerce them to remain in the situation of exploitation. For all this, not just awareness raising conferences, but investigative research is imperative.

For a *relevant response*, an alert and gender sensitive awareness among, not just the NGOs, but also the *different sectors* of civil society is absolutely necessary. Besides, government intervention and support is absolutely essential. The *police force* needs to be sensitized and mobilised to apprehend the culprits, and the *Special Public Prosecutor* must relentlessly pursue the conviction, because there are many loopholes in the law.

GOAN GIRL FACES HARROWING ORDEAL (HERALD DECEMBER 10.2004)

Vasco, December 9, when twenty-four year old Flory Nevidita D'Souza of Fortawaddo in Betim opted to take up house-work in Kuwait, show was hopeful of a bright future. Instead, she was mercilessly beaten black and blue by her boss when she refused to be drawn into prostitution and after repeated death threats barely got away with her life, after relatives paid a huge sum to secure her release.

Flory returned to Goa on that, shattered by the harrowing experiences of her ordeal in Kuwait, but is relieved to have got out alive. Speaking to Herald at her residence in Betim, Flory narrated her ordeal which she said began shortly she glanced upon an advertisement by a travel and manpower resources company in Vasco in early November. "The agent one, Adam, assured me a job on a payment of Rs. 30,000 of which Rs. 21,500 would have to paid in advance," recalled Flory. "I left from Bangalore because I was told that I could not go from Goa, Mumbai or Chennai. Besides me, there were seven other girls from Chennai, Sri Lanka and Indonesia. I was the only Goan in the batch," explained Flory.

She left Bangalore on November 6 and arrived in Hawally–Kuwait the next day, only to realize, to her shock, the job brief that lay in store for her. "In Goa, I was told that I would be doing housework in Kuwait. But when I reached there, I was asked to 'work' with boys," said Flory. I said 'no'. I told my boss that I can work for 24 hours, but I do not want to be with the boys. Flory reminded her boss that the agent Adam in Goa had told her that she would be expected to do housework. "But my boss Shaikh Abdul Kadar told me that what Adam said meant nothing and that, I would have to do what he (the boss) says," Flory added.

My Boss insisted that "I would have to make contact with

boys. When I refused, both Kadar and his wife began beating me with belts and pipes," recalled Flory. The numerous scars on her back, head, hands and legs, bear silent testimony to the torture Flory had to undergo, because she refused to join a prostitution racket. Doomed with no way out, Flory's tiny ray of hope was to come from her family members in Goa who were anxious of her well-being. "When there was no news from my side, my mother in Goa contacted my sister in London, who in turn got in touch with Kadar's family. They demanded cash of Rs. 35,000, so that I would be allowed to go back to Goa." Said Flory.

Other family members too got involved in a desperate bid to secure her release. "My sister contacted my cousin in Kuwait, who spoke to Kadar and assured that the amount of Rs. 35,000 would be paid to them and that, I should not be assaulted," Flory added. "He (Kadar) started demanding money to allow me to return to Goa. Anthony, one of my family members in Kuwait, came to my rescue and promised to pay the Kadar family the amount. The Kadar family was however determined that Flory had to make contact with boys." One day, they even took me to a secluded area and threatened to kill me. I pleaded with them, "Please don't kill me. I am the eldest in the family and I have four other sisters'," recalled Flory, as she fought back the tears.

"They brought me back to the house and tied my neck with a rope. I again began begging with them and told them to leave me. I told them that they could kill me only after taking me to my Mother," she added.

The death threats did not stop there. "The next day in the house, they doused me with kerosene and I repeated my pleas. They then took me to a club and asked me to dance with the boys. When I refused, they said that it was only to give me a good sleep. After I drank the concoction, I felt asleep. They also gave me an injection and took away my belongings, my gold chain and my rings. The other seven girls often used to entertain boys and I was the only one who refused to carry out the orders," informed Flory.

A sum of Rs. 35,000 was then paid by Anthony to free Flory from the clutches of her boss in Kuwait. Only then did they release her, promoting Flory to take the next flight home. She returned to Betim on that morning. Incidentally, it was only at the Dabolim airport that Flory learnt of the fake Emigration Clearance Not Required (ECNR) stamp on her passport." I learnt that my passport had a fake ECNR only after the immigration authorities at Dabolim airport checked my passport. I was informed by immigration authorities that the fake ECNR was manipulated before I left for Kuwait," she said. At present, her passport is in possession of immigration authorities.

Despite the severe physical and mental trauma, Flory did not want to seek justice in the matter. "I do not wish to lodge a formal complaint because I was told that I was at fault for using a fake ECNR stamp," explained Flory. But her decision to decline police intervention only added to her anguish. "I went to the doctors at Goa Medical College Hospital at Bambolim to do so, since there was no police complaint," informed Flory, "Even a private medical practitioner refused to entertain me as there is no Police complaint. I was asked to return to the GMC for a checkup," she added.

Our staff reporter (Gomantak Times December 11, 2001)

Panaji: They were treated worse than a dog. They cooked a few kilos of meat for the canine in the house. But their own food, whatever little they cooked with fire wood, was usually rice without curry and boiled vegetables. The dog was pampered but they badly abused and assaulted. Suravi and Prabhati have a priest and some child rights activists to thank for their freedom from six months of confinement on International Human Rights Day.

A police team accompanied by a NGO members rescued the two sisters from Orissa from a family in Calangute in whose house the minor girls were in humanly treated and exploited. It was not only domestic work which they had to do, but any work that was needed to be done at the hotel the family was running. If their dawn-to-dusk duties were routine, they would not know what they would be asked to do off and on. Sweeping, mopping, washing utensils, cooking food, washing all the linen of the hotel, the list was endless.

Looking pale and haggard, the girls were presented before reporters at a briefing organized by All India Trade Union Congress. They were dressed in clothes which were torn and unwashed for days. Their hands shoed traces of paint and were bleeding from the endless chores. "Often they would be woken up close to midnight and asked to do some chore," Shanti Maria Fonseca of AITUC's child rights cell said speaking to reporters yesterday.

The owner who is a manager of an insurance company in Panaji, and also runs a hotel in Calangute—at present there are nine foreign tourists staying in it—pampered her dog but beat up the two sisters often. The Family has a huge German Shepard dog. The dogs get meat, rice and milk but the girls had to cook their own their own food, which was mostly tasteless. Fonseca further said that a priest Fr. Vijay of National Domestic Workers Movement, Goa unit, cane to know about the sad case of the two minors and informed AITUE about it and the NGO moved the machinery to rescue them.

The sisters from Orissa whose age is 10 and 12 were fourth and fifth standard students back home. But not much is known as to how they landed in Calangute in June this year. "Neighbours accompanied the girls to the police jeep with tears of joy and relief in their eyes," Fonseca said. She said they wanted to prevent the girls from being sent to Bal Niketan as they are treated badly in the remand home at Merces.

Mystery Shrouds Minor Maid's Death at Verna

Our Staff Reporter (Gomantak Times August 20, 2005)

Margao: Geeta Gangawa Laxman Alawle, a nine year old girl, who was working as a maid with a family at Poriebhat, Verna died under tragic circumstances after suffering 94 per cent burn injuries. The mother of the deceased, a labourer has been deserted by her husband and is staying in a slum behind a cinema hall for the past eight years. She hails from Basragy, Karnataka and has two more daughters and a son, all minors. The deceased was one of the twins.

It was poverty that compelled the mother to send her daughter to her daughter to the house of one Domenic Martins to work as maid. She met Martins when the latter was working in a government office in Margao. Gangawa said that her daughter had been sent to the family with a promise of being well looked after and that she had not demanded any salary from Martins. Though the daughter had been working for a year with the family, the mother alleged that she had been complaining of being thrashed by Martins wife, Filomena. She further alleged that her daughter may have been murdered. Around three months back, the girl had returned home and complained of being harassed.

The mother claims that on Monday at 1 p.m., she received a phone call from Martins that her daughter had suffered burn injuries. She immediately rushed to Verna. At the Verna church, she met Martins who took Gangawa on his two-wheeler to his house, where she saw her daughter had suffered burn injuries. She immediately rushed to Verna. At the Verna church, she met Martins who took Gangawa on his to wheeler to his house, where she saw her daughter being taken to GMC hospital.

The mother has claimed that her daughter had disclosed to her that a man caught her from behind and someone poured kerosene on her. She was set afire and later bathed in a sink outside the house. The child's mother claimed that her daughter told her that Filomena kept on shouting that she (Geeta) should suffer and die. Expressing suspicion about Filomena's involvement, the mother says that she did not even bother to console her, though her husband did when she way crying for her daughter.

Meanwhile, Bailancho Ekvott convenor, Auda Viegas who is helping the police said that she was to at all convinced about the explanation offered by the Martins. She said that she visited the site and found a small plastic pot with some kerosene and three match boxes at different places. Though her legs were not hurt or burnt, one of her chappals was totally burned. Viegas demanded that the couple be booked forcing the minor to commit suicide for exploiting and abusing the child. The victim's mother as well as Viegas said that they would not take possession of the deceased unless the couple is arrested.

Two Years Later She Opens can of Worm Against the Martins

Panaji: After two years, the blemishes on her face have cleared somewhat, but the scars in her heart have only grown deeper. Reema (name changed) is trying to discover her childhood innocence that she had lost trying to fulfill her responsibilities towards her family.

Absolutely silent for the last two years, now she had gathered guts to talk against the ill treatment meted against her by the Martins when she was working with them as a maid in Poriebhat, Verna. After Geeta's death, who died under tragic circumstances after suffering 94 per cent burn injuries, and who was working as a maid with a couple, Reema decided to speak about experiences to the police once approached by Bailancho Ekvott. "She was brave and just said, "would have been in her place." Revealed Auda Viegas, Bailancho Ekvott.

After she gave her statement to Verna police, she had been kept at a safe place to ensure that the Domnic and Philomena Martins who were booked under the Goa Children's Act, but are now out of jail, do not harm Reema.

According to Auda, nine year old Reema was employed by the Martins. "Her mother, a widow, sold combs and other items on the footpath. One day, Domnic approached the mother and told her that he wanted to hire his daughter to work in this house. As the mother was in a helpless situation she agreed. In return Domnic gave Reema's mother a small place to stay in Khareband," revealed Auda. "They ill-treated and harassed Reema. Several times she went to sleep on an empty stomach, she was often punished for no fault of hers. For her Rs. 200 she was asked to cook, wash utensils, besides taking care of the small children," said Auda.

She revealed that the girl alleged that once Philomena brought burning coal in a plate and put Reema's hands in it. "When she screamed for help in pain, Philomena was unaffected and didn't stop the torture. Finally, another person who was present in her house rescued her," she informed.

According to Auda, tired with the hatrocities, the child finally ran away from the martins' house and went home to be with her mother. "But her mother coaxed her to return to Martin's house. She was scared that Domnic would throw them out of the house and then they would have no place to stay," she said.

Further, Auda said that the girl even admitted before the Verna police that when Philomena was not at home, Domnic used to touch her private parts and force her to massage his back, even though she refused. "Reema revealed that Domnic tried to get physical with her, while Philomena used to hit her with a stick," said Auda. She added, "Ultimately tired she ran away from the house, took shelter in a church and was finally sent to her mother's house".

But Philomena refuted the charges against her and her husband. She said, "Someone must have forcibly got her to lodge a complaint against us. This girl wanted to work at our place again, and for sometime she pestered us to employ her, but we told her that we already have someone to work for us." She added, "My husband lies to play with children and would play with her also. Her allegations against my husband are baseless. She was only nine years old when she was with us and my husband would never do such a thing to a child."

FACTSHEETS ON GENDER ISSUES

Trafficking in Women and Children

Gender Issues Fact Sheet 2

Downloadable Versions of this Page are Available in Both word format (111 kb) and Acrobat Format (115 kb).

"The effective suppression of trafficking in women and girls for the sex trade is a matter of pressing international concern...the use of women in international prostitution and trafficking networks has become a major focus on international organized crime...Women and girls who are victims of this international trade are at an increased risk of further violence, as well as unwanted pregnancy and sexually transmitted infection, including infection with HIV/AIDS." [Beijing Platform for Action, chap. I, resolution 1, annex ii, para. 122].

Concept of Trafficking

The definition of trafficking and the exploitation and prostitution of others is set out in Articles 1 and 2 of the 1949 Convention for the Suppression on the Traffic in Persons and of the Exploitation of the Prostitution of Others. The Convention refers to actions at both the national and international levels. Since 1949, the concept of trafficking has been extended to include trafficking for the purpose of other forms of exploitation of women. This wider view of trafficking is reflected in the Beijing Declaration and Platform for Action, which also includes forced marriages and forced labour within the concept.

Trafficking and Prostitution—a Development Issue

Trafficking in women and children is clearly a both a human rights and a development issue. Apart from the human, social and economic costs of the sex industry, the spread of venereal diseases and HIV/AIDs, child prostitution deprives children of the opportunity to pursue education and to achieve their full potential. It thus deprivers the national of vital human resources for development. This should be a particular concern in a country such as Thailand that has an adult population with comparatively low levels of education but a rapidly increasing demand for an educated and skilled labour force.

Prostitution has often been seen as a development problem from the supply side. That is, it is argued that young women and girls are forced (or pressured) into the sex industry by poverty and a lack of alternative employment and income-earning opportunities.

Increasingly, prostitution and trafficking are also being seen as a development issue from the demand side. The demand for the services of prostitutes and for women to be trafficked, both within this region and to developed countries, is clearly a function of development. It is a function of both the level of development, which creates both supply and demand, and the nature of that development:

- Development projects in comparatively undeveloped regions and countries often bring with them a rapid increase in the demand for commercial sex due to the sharp increase in the numbers of unaccompanied male workers in areas where there are few outlets for recreation and entertainment.
- Patterns of development that depend heavily on temporary migrant workers, particularly male workers, are likely to be associated with a sharp increase in the demand for commercial sex.
- Marked differences in income levels within the region contribute to a strong demand for women and children to be trafficked from low income countries to high income countries where the income to be gained from prostitution by the procurers is many times greater than in the country of origin.
- The increasing ease and frequency of international travel, together with the growing phenomenon of temporary migration for work, has increased the opportunities for trafficking.
- The growth of transactional crime involved in a variety of forms of trafficking, including of drugs, has led to the expansion of these networks into trafficking for the purpose of prostitution and other forms of exploitation.

Strategies for Combatting Trafficking

Government agencies and NGOs, together with the international community, have adopted a variety of strategies to combat trafficking in women and children. These include:

- Prevention of trafficking through the legal and criminal system, training of law enforcement officers.
- Control and suppression of prostitution through the legal system.
- Rescue and rehabilitation for women and girl victims of trafficking.
- Protection for and awareness-raising among women and girls to prevent trafficking.
- Demand reduction through advocacy to raise public awareness, particularly in relation to forced and child prostitution and other measures.
- Supply reduction by advocacy and awareness-raising among parents and guardians.
- Supply reduction through the provision of alternative employment and income-earning opportunities for women and girls.
- Supply reduction through campaigns targeting parents on the long-term advantages of girls education.

Data on Trafficking and Prostitution

There are almost no reliable estimates of the number of women who are trafficked or on form where and to where they are trafficked. Trafficking is not reported as such as a category in the crime statistics collected by the United Nations, However, many countries are beginning to collect information on the phenomenon. The Government of Nepal estimated that in 1992 not less than 200,000 Nepalese women and girls were working in brothels in India. A considerable number had been either forcefully abducted or tricked into going to India and had been sold to brothels, [United Nations, 1996: page 7, paras 15-18].

In Thailand, the only estimates available relate to prostitution. A significant proportion of prostitutes, including most child prostitutes, are either forced or tricked into the trade

Estimates of the numbers of prostitutes in Thailand vary widely, depending on the source of the figures and the method of estimation. In 1995, the Public Health Ministry estimated that there were 81,384 Commercial Sex Workers (CSWs) of whom 16,383 were direct CSWs and 65,001 indirect CSWs. The total number of brothels was reported as 6,53, 1,799 of these being outright brothels and the remainder places where prostitutes were available but not the main business. These business figures were based on a twice yearly survey of sex establishments related to surveillance of venereal diseases.

The Police Department provides the highest estimate of the numbers of CSWs – 500,000 based on the number of registered entertainment places. The National Commission on Women's Affairs estimated the number to be 150,000 to 200,000, of whom not more than 20 per cent were thought to be children. Academics from the Population and Social Research Institute of Mahidol University estimated the numbers to be between 200,000 and 300,000.

By contrast, NGOs working on children's rights issues estimate the number of prostituted children to range between 200,000 (ECPAT 1994) and 800,000 (CENTRE FOR Protection of Children's Rights CPCR, 1989). The latter figure seems too high, implying that one of every 4 females aged 11 to 17 was a prostitute. However, in defence of the estimate, the figure includes not only Thai children but also those from the northern hill tribe minorities, Burmese, Chinese, Lao and Cambodian children who are trafficked into Thailand's sex industry. [Caye, 1995: 30-33].

Voluntary or Forced Entry to Prostitution

Three modes of entry into prostitution have been identified:

- *Voluntary* indicates that the woman, prostitute-to-be, approaches the owner/manager of a sex establishment herself;
- *Bounded* implies the involvement of parents or guardians who receive money from an agency or owner for giving

away their daughter;

- *Involuntary* involves the use of deception and coercion of the women by an agent or owner/manager.

However, the distinctions between them are not as clear as the definitions might suggest. "Voluntary" does not necessarily mean free choice or informed consent. Interviews with victims of child prostitution in Thai NGO shelters revealed that many girls who said that they "knew" they would be working as prostitutes actually did not know what that meant. They thought that it meant "wearing Western clothes in a restaurant." Many also said that they could leave the brothels freely but when asked if they had ever tried, most said that had not dared because they had no money of because they feared being arrested or sold to another brothel. Most also said that they could refuse a customer, but further questioning revealed that refusal was virtually unheard of because of the fear of repercussions. [Caye, 1995: 25]

Cultural Context of Prostitution in the Mekong Region

There are cultural, familial, economic and historical reasons behind the decision to send a child to work in the sex industry. In Thailand and neighbouring countries children are expected to support and obey parents' wishes, and show parents gratitude and respect no matter what the difficulties. Many children who migrate to Thailand to work in difficult, low-paid and dangerous occupations feel that they should not return home "empty handed" due to their traditional responsibility to care for their parents. Prostitution is often perceived as fulfilling a traditional role of daughters who are caretakers of the family and community. Under Theravda Buddhism, women and girls are thought to be unable to achieve enlightenment. Thus, while men can show gratitude and respect to their parents by becoming monks and pursuing the spiritual life, many girls feel that they must make sacrifices for the benefit of their families, villages and their own farma, [Caye, 1995: 26-27]

International Legal Instruments

"International Law clearly condemns slavery and slave-related practices. It is well established that the prohibition of these practices has attained the status of customary international law." [Human Watch Rights Watch, 1993: 29]

Convention for the Suppression of Traffic in Person of the Exploitation of the Prostitution of Others (The Trafficking Convention)

The international community first denounced trafficking in the Trafficking Convention, which was approved by the General Assembly of the United Nations in 1949. The convention calls on states parties to punish traffickers and to protect all persons against such abuse. It also calls on states parties "so far as possible" to "make suitable provisions for [trafficking victims] temporary care and maintenance" to repatriate trafficked persons "only after agreement...with the State of destination", and where such persons cannot pay the cost of repatriation, to bear the cost "as far as the nearest frontier". [Convention for the Suppression of the Traffic in Persons, Article 19]. Thailand has not ratified the Trafficking Convention. The convention deals only with trafficking for the purposes of prostitution, and is now regarded by many NGOs as out-of-date.

Convention on the Elimination for All Forms of Discrimination Against Women

Under CEDAW, states parties are obliged to eliminate discrimination and must take all appropriate measures to suppress all forms of traffic in women (Articles 2e and 6). However, the convention does not explain what these measures might be. Thailand ratified CEDAW in 1985, with reservations on Articles 7, 9, 19, 11, 15, 16 and 29. Some reservations were recently withdrawn.

Some countries have expressed concern that although the Convention itself does not require that acts of prostitution be criminalized, several of its provisions have the indirect effect of making the practice of prostitution illegal. Australia, for example, noted that these provisions blur the distinction between voluntary and coerced prostitution. "To consider voluntary sex work and coercive prostitution as the same issue, and therefore to demand the outlaw of prostitution per se, is to view prostitution as a moral issue and to consider sex workers as people unable to make informed decisions on their life. Such as view is paternalistic and raises serious human rights implications. Further, criminalization of the voluntary sex industry fosters conditions of violence against women sex workers," [United Nations, 1996, pages 8- 9, para 26].

Convention on the Rights of the Child 1989 (CRC)

The CRC defines the child as a person under 18 years of age, unless the national laws recognise a younger age of majority. States parties are obliged to protect children from all forms of discrimination (Article 2), to protect them from sexual exploitation and abuse, including prostitution and pornography (Article 34) and to make every effort to prevent the sale, trafficking and abduction of children (Article 35). Under Article 39, states parties have an obligation to ensure that victims of exploitation receive appropriate treatment for their recovery and social reintegration. Thailand acceded to the CRC in 1992.

Thai Legal Instruments

The Trafficking in Women and Girls Act (Anti-Trafficking Act) of 1928

The Anti-Trafficking Act was passed in 1928 as a result of the perceived increase in numbers of foreign nationals in Thai brothels. It prohibits trafficking in women and girls. Section 7 states that women and girls who have been trafficked into Thailand will be exempt from imprisonment and/or fines. However, before being deported they must be sent to a state reform house for 30 days, a period which can be extended by a judge. The Anti-Trafficking Law also requires Thai authorities to arrange and shoulder the cost of the victim's repartriation to her country of origin. [Caye, 1995: 1]

The Suppression of Prostitution Act of 1960

The Suppression of Prostitution Act (Prostitution Prohibition Act) was passed in 1960 partly as the result of UN pressure. The Act replaced the Contagious Diseases Prevention Act, 1908, which aimed to control prostitution. The new law was intended to eliminate prostitution (defined as an act promiscuously rendering sexual services for remuneration) by making it an illegal activity. The Act provided that convicted prostitutes should be reformed through medical treatment and a period not exceeding one year in an assistance centre where they were to receive vocational training. [Caye, 1995: -2] This Act was repealed by the new Prevention and Suppression of Prostitution Act of 1996.

The Entertainment Places Act of 1966

This act was designed to pave the way for brothels to be legalized in the guise of massage parlours, bars, night-clubs, tea-houses etc. It was enacted at a time when the Government sought to increase state revenue from the "Rest and Recreation" activities of the US armed forces stationed in Vietnam. The Act defines the various kinds of "Entertainment Places" and allows such places to operate only under a license to be obtained from local police stations. The use of licensed establishments for prostitution is illegal. The Act sets 18 years as the minimum age for women to work in such establishments but the penalty for employing under-age women in only bath 2,000. [Caye, 1995: 2].

The Penal Code of 1956

Under the Thai Penal Code 1956, prostitution is not illegal but procurement for the purpose of prostitution is. The Penal Code imposes more severe penalties for procurement than the Prostitution Prohibition Act. Several sections provide specific and quite harsh punishment for abuses against girls forced into prostitution, penalties that increase if the girl is under 18 years of age and increase still further for offences against girls under 15 and 13 years of age. Section 276 penalises forced sexual intercourse with a women "who is not wife, against her will, by threatening her by any means whatever" with 4 to 20 years imprisonment and a fine of 8,000 to 40,000 bath. Section 277 makes sexual intercourse with a girl under 15 statutory rape, even if with her consent. [Caye, 1995: 3-4].

The Thai Immigration Act of 1979

The Thai Immigration Act denies entry to Thailand to those who have engaged in prostitution, trading in girls and other immoral activities. Any person who "brings or takes an alien into the Kingdom...shall be imprisoned for not more than 10 years or fined not more than 100,000.

Prevention and Suppression of Prostitution Act of 1996

The new Act defines prostitution "accept sexual act or accept other action or anything for the sexual satisfaction of other person for the benefit of pay or other interest," irrespective of the sex of the recipient or the prostitute. The Act continues make to prostitution illegal but considerably reduces the penalties for the prostitute. In addition, if the prostitution is forced then the prostitute is not deemed to have committed an offence.

The new provisions of the act are:

- the clients of a prostitute under the age of 18 also commit an offence punishable by imprisonment;
- parents or guardians who collaborate in the prostitution of a child under the age of 18 commit an offence publishable by a fine and revocation of guardianship;
- those involved in forced prostitution will be punished by a term of imprisonment from 10 to 20 years and a fine from 200,000 to 4000,000 baht.
- in the event of serious injury of death to the victim, the penalty shall be life imprisonment or death. [Government Gazette, Vol. 113, part 54 a, page 1, dated 22 October 2539 International Translations Office, Vo.. 51. No. 2 (February 1997).
- All prostitutes under age 18 shall received protection and vocational development for up to 2 years;

- Requires the establishment of a Committee for Protection and vocational Development at the national level and in each province;
- The private sector, foundations and NGOs working in the area can apply to the authority to establish a primary shelter or a centre for protection and vocational development.

REFERENCES

Human Rights Watch, 1993. *A Modern Form of Slavery: Trafficking of Burmese Women and Girls into Brothels in Thailand.* Asia Watch and Women' rights Project.

United Nations, Advancement of Women. Traffic in women and girls. Report of the Secretary-General. General Assembly Document A/51/309 27 August, 1996.

CHAPTER-5

Perspectives and Realities of Women Prostitution

Earlier it has been given religious sanction by dedicating girls to a deity or deities gradually it has changed to a commercial business due to changes in human beings living conditions. Now it has been a great social evil, which has severely affect the health, personality, family and the society. It passes dangerous disease like veneral disease, syphilis and acquired ammuno deficiency syndrom (Aids) from one person to another and it affects his or her spouse and children to be born. There are research studies conduced on prostitution and have found that those who indulge into prostitution may get defective children. Such as blind, deaf and dump etc. It has been estimated that in U.S.A. 25 per cent of all blindness is transmitted by infected mothers to the unborn foetus. Elliot and Merrill have observed that even real disease produced a large share of insanity and its victims are particularly prone to commit violent crimes and result of its injections create major public health problems. The Hindustan Times of October 22, 1991, New Delhi reported that Indian Health Organisation survey, a massive 52 percent of urban youths (aged between 14 to 18 years) had already had their sexual experience, a majority of them in the red light areas, where they constituted nearly 30 per cent of the clientele, thereby becoming easy victims of the dreadful Human Immuno deficiency Virus HIV) that causes AIDS. Aids destroys the body's ability to fight disease. International health authorities estimate that tens of thousands of people have died world wide due to the disease which no effective cure has been found as yet.

Factors of Prostitution

The Prostitute population is reported by Illustrated Weekly of India, dated 26th November, 1972, these were over 6,000 professional (among them about 1,500 call girls) and at least 2,000 brothels spread allover the city of Delhi." According to the Sunday of 21-27 July 1991, on the number of prostitutes in Mumbai very from 50,000 to 5,00,000. Mumbai has the largest red light area (prostitutes) in the world. There are many factors that affect young girls and women who indulge into prostitution. Economic factor is lone of the major factors, which force them to enter into prostitution. Boner observes that economic factors responsible for underprivileged girls entering prostitution are immoral environments, early employment and poverty....Inadequate housing and lack of privacy, which compel the children to sleep in the same room wit other elders, endanger their morality. Early employment brings close contact with immoral influences, through other working men and women who attire them into techniques and practices of promiscuous sex relationship. Absolute poverty compel many girls to rush to prostitution to enable to live. Relative poverty resulting in lack of many of the small luxuries, lead to prostitution to attain these.

Religious practice of Devadasi systems is still prevailing since third century A.D. It was prevalent in various forms in ancient civilizations of Bobylon, Egypt, Arabia, Greece, syris and other parts of Central Asia. It has been also got strong roots in Andhra Pradesh, Karnataka, Tamil Nadu and Maharashtra though it has been banned legally. In these states girls are dedicated to temples for singing and dancing. There are other factors namely unemployment, rapid urbanisation, kidnapping, films, drinking, bad company unsatisfactory drugs, home conditions, immoral character of either parents and improper supervision in the family etc. Thus, in order to prevent prostitution, the government has enacted the immoral Traffic (Prevention) act, 1956. Previously known as Suppression of Immoral Traffic in Women and Girls Act. 1956. Under this act, punishment for keeping a brothel or allowing premises to be used as a brothels pimps, procuring inducing or taking (person) for the sake of prostitution and carries of prostitution in the prohibited area As per this Act, carrying on prostitution within he distance of two hundred meters of any place of public religious worship, educational institutional, hostel, hospital, nursing home or such other public place of any kind as may be notified in this behalf by he commissioner and police of magistrate in the manner prescribed. It provides that the special police officer/trafficking police officers, and that a woman/girl would be interrogated only by a women police officer and in their non-availability, in the presence of woman social worker. The bonafides of those coming forward to take custody of the rescued victim, must now be investigated by a recognized welfare institution or organisation before she is released.. Provision is made for police officers to deal with offences of interstate ramifications when dealing with trafficking compulsory medical examination of those rescued and their rehabilitation are also provided for.

The girl child is always prone to sexual exploitation and abuse even within the four walls of her house. Amazingly, even father found rapists of daughters as frequently flashed in news by media. Relatives, including close blood relations, family visitors, acquaintance, friends, neighbours, tutors, etc., not only entice and reduce to play with the modesty of innocent girls but also remain in search of lonely occasions when they are able to force them to surrender and submit to their lust for several pleasure. In a study conducted by the Family Planning Association of India, 68 parent of the women covered in the survey were found to have disclosed that "They had been the victims of sexual molestation by their older male relatives when they were children. Many others had been molested by neighbours, family friends and occupational visitors, sometimes even teachers and doctors. Criminals committing rapes and other sexual crimes against women generally are characterized by immoral behaviour of the norms of social interactions and unhealthy family relations. Views and attitudes of social roles of women and to sexual relations typical to criminals of this kind are incompatible, with the existing and generally recognized morals. It is surprise to note that for fear of society and insults a victim of rape may prefer to remain silent, thus giving a change to the accused who in many cases is a rich, landlord, influential man in the society. Rapes are always committed intentionally with proper planning. In 1973, volume of rape per lakh of population was only 0.5 whereas it reaches to 0.8 in 1983. However, the percentage of rape under important I.P.C. crime heads remain constant from 1980 till 1983. The Law Commission had in its 84th report on Rape and Allied Offences proposed certain changes in the Indian Penal Code, the Code of Criminal Procedure and the Code of Criminal Procedure and the Indian Evidence Act. On the basis of these recommendations, the Government amended the law on the rape and introduced the Criminal Law (Amendment) bill in 1980, which was ultimately passed as an Act in1983.

Section 366 of IPC

Kidnapping, Abducting or Inducing Women to compel her Marriage, etc. Whoever kidnaps or abduct any woman with intent that she may be compelled, or knowing it to be likely that she will be compelled, to marry any person against her will, or in order that she may be forced or seduced to illicit intercourse, shall be punished with imprisonment of either description for a term which may extend to ten years, and shall also be liable to fine; and whoever, by means of criminal intimidation as defined in this ode or of abuse of authority or any other method of compulsion, induces any women to go from any place with intent that she may be, or knowing tat it is likely that she will be, forced or seduced to illicit intercourse with another person, shall also be punishable as aforesaid.

Section 366-A of IPC

Procuration of Minor Girl

Whoever, by any means whatsoever, induces any minor girl under the age of eighteen years to go from any place or to do any act with intent that such girl may be, knowing that its is likely that she will be, forced or seduced to illicit intercourse with another person, shall be punishable with imprisonment which may extend to ten years, and shall also be liable to fine.

Section 366-B of IPC

Whoever imports into India from any country outside India or from the State of Jammu and Kashmir any girl under the age of twenty-one years within tent that she may be, or knowing it to be likely that she will be, forced or seduced to illicit intercourse with another person shall be punishable with imprisonment which may extent to ten years, and shall also be liable to fine.

Section 372-A of IPC

Selling Minor for Purpose of Prostitutions etc.

Whoever sells, lets to hire, or otherwise disposes of any person under the age of eighteen years with intent that such person shall at any age be employed or used for the purpose of prostitution or illicit intercourse with any person or for any unlawful and immoral purpose, or knowing it to likely that such person will at any age be employed or used for any such purpose, shall be punished with imprisonment of either description for a term which may extend to ten years, and shall also be liable to fine.

Explanation 1. When a female under the age of eighteen years is sold, let for hire, or otherwise disposes of to a prostitute or to any person who keeps or manages a brothel, the person sol disposing of such female shall, until the contrary is proved, presumed to have disposed of her with the intent that she shall be used for the purpose of prostitution.

Explanation II. For the purposes of this section "illicit intercourse" men sexual intercourse between persons not united by marriage, or by any union or tie which, though not amounting to a marriage, is recognized by the personal law or custom of the community to which they belong or, where they belong to different communities, or both such communities, as constituting between them a quasi-material relation.

Section 373 of IPC

Buying Minor for Purposes of Prostitutions etc.

Whoever buys, hires or otherwise obtains possession of any person under the age of eighteen years with intent that such person shall at any age be employed or used for the purpose of prostitution or illicit intercourse with any person or for any unlawful and immoral purpose, or knowing it to be likely that such person will at any age be employed or used for an such purpose, shall be punished with imprisonment of either description for a term which may extend to ten years, and shall also be liable to fine.

Explanation I. – Any prostitute or any person keeping or managing a brothel, who buys, hires or otherwise obtains possession of a female under the age of eighteen years shall, until the contrary is proved, be presumed to have obtained possession of such female with the intent that she shall be used for the purpose of prostitution.

Explanation II. –"Illicit intercourse" has the same meaning as in Section 372.

The state protective homes or corrective institutions in which the reused person kept are known for their poor living conditions with no rehabilitation programmes except marriage, which is treated as their ultimate destiny. This requires sympathetic effort and care by the State Governments which could involves voluntary organisations in running or supervising these institutions and linking up with available training and rehabilitation programmes. Some of the Voluntary Organisations especially working for there habilitation of prostitutes and their children inside Maharashtra and Karnataka etc., and are utilizing benefits from these services.

Raja Ramomohan Roy, Maharshi Karve, Mahatma Phule, Mahatma Gandhi and Dr. Ambedkar and M.G. Ranade are among the great social reformer in India who have made concerted efforts for the eradication of social evils that plague our society lay in women's education and economic liberation. Though we have equality of status, rights and privileges legally and constitutionally bestowed upon women. She has been traditionally been put in a weak position. There is often a wide gap between the legislative intent and the use of laws and legal processes in reality.

While Parliament and State Legislatures respond to public opinion by enacting legislation conducive to the attainment of equality, considerable time is lost in framing rules, appointment of functionaries, setting up legal institution, etc. the personnel of the legal system can influence the progress of the law. Though more women are getting into the judicial and police administration, there is always the danger that they would be absorbed into the traditional side of justice administration bringing little change in the situation. This calls for a greater, more widespread, and planned interaction between functionaries of justice administration on the one hand and social activists and researchers on the other. With these cautionary words, let us examine the type of services that should be made available to women o improve on and enforce their legal rights. Their social, educational and financial hardship make women specially vunerable when facing problems within the family, such as matrimonial conflicts which compel them to resort to law. Hence, bearing these aspects in mind, the programmes of legal services for women should include.

Special programmes forgiving information to women regarding their legal rights; this may even involve regarding their legal rights; this may even involved reaching out to such women as e.g., women in Jails, women in mental asylums, women in purdah—and initiating legal action on their behalf.

Identifying special problems of women and reaching out to women indeed for help.

Giving relevant information to women regarding their legal rights; this may include giving of talks of the use of the media, printing and distribution of pamphlets or articles giving relevant information in simple language.

Availability of free or subsidized legal advice as also services of a lawyer of her choice to a women litigant in a deserving case.

Filing test cases, class action or public interest action in suitable cases.

If was are unsatisfactory, creating a lobby for suitable law reforms.

A Programme for advice and conciliation in family dispute— under which the parties to the dispute can be summoned, their problem discussed by trained family counsellors and reconciliation attempted.

An emergency call where women in urgent need of help can go and if necessary, stay for sometime as also receive legal advice and help e.g., women who are subjected to physical abuse, women harassed for money or dowry by their in-laws, women thrown out of their matrimonial homes, women who want protection for their children who are physically abused and so on.

An information desk where apart form legal information women in distress can get information about women' homes and hostels where they can stay with their children if required and regarding any jobs or training in work available to them.

Effective implementation of relevant laws can check the crimes against women to a great extent. Current trends in degradation of social morality, corruption, bribery, fashion materialistic attitude are mainly responsible for such crime.

Commercial Child Sexual Abuse in India

Making people commodities, literally, has never before reached the proportions as in the world today, not under slavery, not in feudal times. UNICEF estimates that worldwide, at least one million children are trapped in the sex trade, most of them girls between 10 and 16 years of age. According to a 1998 report of the DWCD around 30 per cent of the sex workers in India are below 18 years of age, while 40 per cent were inducted into the trade as minors. However, the Joint Women's Programme (JWP), a Delhi-based women's organisation, has put the ratio of under-16 sex workers at a high of 68 per cent.

The Protocol to Prevent, Suppress and Punish Trafficking in Persons, Especially Women and Children, supplementing the United Nations Convention against Transnational Crime, 2000, defines trafficking as: "The recruitment, transportation, transfer, harbouring or receipt of persons, by means of the threat or use of force or other forms of coercion, of abduction, of fraud, of deception, of the abuse of power or of a position of vulnerability or of the giving or receiving of payments or benefits to achieve the consent of a person having control over another person, for the purpose of exploitation." It further says: "Exploitation shall include, at a minimum, the exploitation of the prostitution of others or other forms of sexual exploitation, forced labour or services, slavery or practices similar to slavery..."

Trafficking is also understood to include "the recruitment, harbouring, transportation, provision, or obtaining of a person for labour or services, through the use of force, fraud or coercion for the purpose of subjection to involuntary servitude, peonage, debt bondage, or slavery.'

The Convention on the Rights of the Child (CRC) defines a child as every human being below the age of 18 years. This is reflected in the UN Convention against Transnational Organised Crime which defines trafficking of children for sexual exploitation as inducing "a commercial sex act...by force, fraud, or coercion,... in which the person induced to perform such act has not attained 18 years of age." It is estimated by international policing agencies that at a minimum, 700,000 persons are trafficked each year across international borders, most of the victims being women and children.

It is believed that the number may be significantly higher. Trafficking occurs across national borders and within countries. As a report on trafficking presented in 2000 said: "It is found in both developed and developing nations, in countries where the government abuses human rights, and in countries where the government's human rights record is generally excellent."

The same report states: "Some victims have answered advertisements believing that they will have a good job awaiting them in a new country. Others have been sold into this modern-day form of slavery by a relative acquaintance, or family friend." Criminal networks take advantage of victim's vulnerability, at the root of which lie poverty, ignorance, often illiteracy, and poor income-generating skills.

Trafficking in persons, including children, is believed to be closely linked to the criminal networks that organise trafficking in drugs and presumably arms. Trafficking of person, including children, for commercial sexual exploitation is often linked to networks involved in organising illegal adoption routes, illegal migration, and illegal marriage arrangement bureaus, or 'mail-order brides' as this has come to be known in East Asia.

Tackling trafficking in children, whether it is for commercial sex or pornography or for labour as in the case of the 'camel jockey' boys, is made all the more difficult as it would mean tackling networks that have links with illegal drugs and arms trading networks. These networks, it is believed, necessarily have political protection or connections, compounding the problem.

India is both a destination and a transit country for traffickers, faced with tackling both inter-province and inter-national trafficking.

While an international survey found no evidence of government complicity with traffickers in South Asia, complicity among police, border, and immigration officials were found to severely undermine law enforcement efforts.

Because of the transnational character of trafficking, combating it requires governments as well as civil society organisations to pull together. Networks, both within countries and across borders, have been set up, largely supported by international organisations such as the United Nations.

Though the goal of eradicating trafficking is still distant, several effective measures are in place... and every successful intervention is a life made more secure.

Unknown Numbers

The numbers of children who become victims of trafficking—for labour, for commercial sexual exploitation or other forms of abuse—are unknown mainly due to the dispersed and clandestine nature of the phenomenon.

The National Crime Records Bureau, Ministry for Home Affairs, Government of India stated that in the five years between 1994 and 1998, reports of buying of minor girls for prostitution has been on the increase...though reported incidence of selling of girls has declined.

Between 5,000 to 10,000 Nepalese children, mostly between the ages of 10 and 18, are trafficked into India annually. Most end up in he sex trade, some become domestic workers.

UNICEF estimates that there are at least a million child prostitutes in Asia alone with the greatest numbers in India, Thailand, Taiwan and the Philippines.

A quarter of the estimated 2.3 million sex workers in India are minors, in over 1,000 sex trade districts all over India.

A study by the Indian Health Association released in 1993, quoted in *Child Trafficking in India* Published by The Haq Foundation in 2001, found that 10 per cent of children engaged in commercial sex are children of sex workers, about 40 per cent had been abducted, five per cent had been victims of rape and eight per cent of incestuous relations.

A GOI / UNICEF strategy appear (Oct 19, 2001) for Programme of Cooperation, 2003-07, states: "it is estimated that in six cities of India there are about 100,000 children who are victims of sexual exploitation. The number is likely to be a gross under-estimate given its limited coverage. Many cities in India have also become the destination for cross-border trafficking of children, primarily for prostitution."

Trafficking and Commercial Child Sexual Abuse in India

"As a signatory to the UN Convention on the Rights of the Child, India ranks among 122 UN member-counties committed to fight trafficking of persons."

The Government of India is currently seriously considering

ratifying the Optional Protocol to the Convention on the Rights of the Child on the Sale of Children, Child Prostitution and Child Pornography, which was adopted by the UN General Assembly in May 2000. It has started the process to ratify the ILO Convention (No. 182) on the Worth Forms of Child Labour (sale and trafficking of children is considered a slavery-like practice and is forbidden by convention 182). The Government is also in the process of ratifying the Protocol to Prevent, Suppress and Punish Trafficking in Persons, Especially Women and Children, a supplementing the United Nations Convention against Transnational Crime.

Within its borders, the Government of India has followed up the World Congress against Commercial Sexual Exploitation of Children at Stockholm by

- Drawing up a National Plan of Action (in 1998) and constituted a National Advisory Committee to combat trafficking, rehabilitate victims of trafficking and commercial sexual exploitation and improve legal and law enforcement systems to strengthen the fight.
- Setting up State Advisory Committees on Trafficking for the same purpose, devolving authority and seeking to mobilise greater State resources in the fight against trafficking
- Reviewing the existing legal framework including the Immoral Trafficking Prevention Act (ITPA), Indian Penal Code (IPC) and enacting the Juvenile Justice Act (JJA) 2000 and the Indian Information Technology Act, 2000 which declares online pornography a punishable offence (Section 67).
- Undertaking regional efforts, in alliance with NGOs, to create greater awareness of the dimensions of trafficking and increase sensitivity to victims among government departments, the police and judiciary, as well as within civil society at large.
- Enacting legislation to prohibit *Devdasi* and *Jogin* traditions of sexual exploitation.
- Profiling NGOs that are engaged in tackling trafficking

and helping to rehabilitate victims.

- Creating schemes of assistance to NGOs to combat trafficking in source areas, traditional areas and destination areas through efforts to prevent, rescue and rehabilitate.
- Initiating a new scheme called SWADHAR for women in difficult situations applicable to victims of trafficking also
- Co-operating with the Asian Developing Bank to conduct a survey on regional cross border trafficking.

In addition, the National Human Rights Commission (NHRC) of India, in association with UNIFEM, has initiated a survey of trafficking, across national boundaries and within the country. The study will also investigate the causal and behavioural aspects of all agents in trafficking.

The NHRC, together with the National Law School, is also engaged in preparing manuals for judicial officials, focusing particularly on the judges at the district and *taluka* (lower administrative block) levels. The Government of India, jointly with UNICEF is simultaneously preparing a similar manual for police personnel. The Government, in association with Tata Institute of Social Sciences, is also creating a manual for training social workers in dealing wit issues of trafficking. Alongside, the Department of Women and Child Development (DWCD) of the Union Government is considering a manual to sensitize medical professionals, against focusing on audiences at the district and *taluka* levels.

But perhaps most significant for those at the ground level, the Government has begun the process of creating a network of special police officers to monitor trafficking.

However, the modalities for setting up a nodal monitoring agency, as suggested by Radhika Coomaraswamy, Special Rapporteur on Human Rights appointed by the UNHCRC, are still being deliberated. The Government is also in the process of finalising the norms for a National Commission for Children and drafting a Policy and Charter for Children, ensuring children's right to survival health and nutrition, care and education...and to be protected from exploitation.

Trafficking for the Global Market Through Sex Tourism and Pornography

In 1991, Freddy Albert Peat a foreigner who had been living in Goa, a tourist haven in peninsular India, for close to 25 years, was arrested NGOs who had suspected Peat's motives in his relationship with young boys, were vindicated. Peat had indeed been using children for pornography and selling young boys to pedophiles.

Peat's connections were found to stretch to Mumbai, Maharashtra, in Western India and beyond the country's shores. He was linked to a pornography network being run by a Swiss couple in Mumbai that the forum Against Child Sexual Exploitation (FACSE) helped expose.

This case has given rise to one of the most active initiatives against trafficking and tourism-related sexual exploitation of children, organized jointly by the Child Right Group, Jagrut Goenkaranchi Fauz, Umed and others, including some, like FACSE, in Maharashtra.

The day that Peat was convicted, in March 1996, was as much a victory of the NGOs as it was of the Calangute policemen, who acted promptly and soon took the lead in building up an effective case that put peats behind bars.

April 4, 1991, the day that Peats was arrested is today observed in Goa as Anti-Child Prostitution Day.

Certain landmark court cases have influenced the government decisions and plans of action, among these the 1990 case of *Vishal Jeet vs. Union of India*, in which the Supreme Court directed the government to undertake steps much in keeping with the Coomaraswamy recommendations that came nearly a decade later. In the 1997 case of *Gaurav Jain vs. Union of India* too, the Supreme Court directives echoed the same sentiments.

The former case led to the government constituting the Central Advisory Committee on child Prostitution in 1994 and the latter to the formation of the Committee on Prostitution, Child Prostitution and Children of Prostitutes in 1997 which formulated the National Plan of Action.

Government and NGOs alike are paying increasing attention

till now to the linkages between poverty and trafficking for purposes other than sexual exploitation. As with trafficking for sexual exploitation, the numbers of victims are not known. The trafficking in young boys as jockeys for camel racing from Bangladesh via India to West Asia is by now well-known, and believed to have been stopped. But the numbers of young women, some below 18, who are illegally transported as domestic help, are only suspected.

Acknowledging Trafficking

The acknowledgement of 'trafficking' itself has been a milestone in some states (provinces), with governments steeped in the tradition of "tackling prostitution", punishing the victims of commercial sexual exploitation as much as the organisers of that exploitation.

Acknowledging that trafficking in children does exist has come on the heels of scandalous revelations in recent times about the smuggling of young boys from Bangladesh to west Asia via India, for camel racing or the October 2001 outrage over a prominent medical practitioner in a southern state being accused or trafficking in babies for adoption.

Such exposures have given a further impetus to the state governments to act to combat trafficking and other violations against children.

While most state governments have appointed committees to draft state-wise policies and action plan, those more concerned with trafficking, either as 'recipients' or 'suppliers' of victims of trafficking networks, are moving ahead noticeably more rapidly. Actions include finalizing rescue' policies, as well as state-level consultations on trafficking and exploitation of children for commercial sex, especially on measures to improve law enforcement.

Initiatives with NGOs are ongoing, principally in community-based programmes for resettlement of victims of trafficking, especially children. These also includes a range of activities for creating social awareness—from making people aware not only of the dimensions of trafficking, but also how to be vigilant against traffickers, to making them sensitive to the plight and needs of victims of trafficking.

With most State Governments actively projecting their provinces as modern, forward-looking and desirable investment destinations, the fact that such an image sits ill alongside criminal networks, including those engaged in trafficking, has become all too clear. This has given an impetus to act quickly and decisively.

Some states are linked to national anti-trafficking networks such as the Action Against Trafficking and Sexual Exploitation of Children (ATSEC), which works closely with the police and the State Departments of Welfare.

Policy Initiatives Against Trafficking

The Immoral Traffic Prevention Act, 1986 (ITPA), a modification of the1956 Suppression of Immoral Traffic in Women and Girls Act (SITA), supplemented by the Indian Penal Code (IPC) prohibits trafficking in persons including children.

The GOI is in the process of finalising amendments to the ITPA. Primarily, the amendments under consideration would make the law sensitive to victims and will make penalties on traffickers more servere. Also under consideration is the amendment to include health protection clauses and steps of prevent trafficking. For this purpose the National Commission for Women (NCW), a statutory body, held countrywide consultations and came out with certain substantial amendments in the Act.

One of the most significant steps taken by the Government is to designate the officers of the Central Bureau of Investigation (CBI) of the rank of inspector and higher, as Trafficking Officers, giving them a special mandate to deal with cases of organised trafficking with Inter State and Inter Country ramifications.

The Government is also working on finalising the modalities of setting up a cell on trafficking and sexual abuse of children within the CBI.

Guidelines on dealing with trafficking have been circulated among all state (provincial) governments. In addition to stipulating the appointment of special police officers briefed to tackle trafficking, the guidelines also lay down that the police should be assisted in this task by an advisory board of social workers and NGOs.

Going Against Tradition, Fighting the Devdasi System

The Delhi-based Joint Women's Programme conducted a study of the traditional *devadasi* system in south India in 1981. What came out of it was not only a horrifying expose of the exploitation of young girls, but ultimately the Karnataka *Devadasis* (Prohibition of Dedication) Act of 1983.

Devdasis – like *jogins, basavis, bhavins, venkatasanis, nailis, muralis, theradiyanis* and others elsewhere in traditional Hindu society– were 'dedicated' to temple gods and subsequently sexually exploited by priests and other high-caste men of the community.

The practice has been legally abolished but is known to be prevalent still. According to a 1996 study by academic Indrani Sinha, scheduled caste families still 'dedicate' over 5,000 girls every year to temple gods and thus yield them over to a life of prostitution and sexual abuse. Most girls are between 10 and 14 years old.

Plans for Action at the State Level: Focus on Rehabilitation

The Union Government has directed State Governments to draft plans for action against trafficking in persons at the state (provincial) levels and has also circulated guidelines (as described above) for these.

According to the National Human Rights Commission and surveys by various NGOs such as the Centre of Concern for Child Labour the following are considered 'high-traffic' states – Andhra Pradesh, Bihar, Karnataka, Maharashtra, Tamil Nadu, Uttar Pradesh and West Bengal. In addition, there is trafficking within what is know as the

'Pink Triangle' (The Delhi-Jaipur (in Rajasthan)-Agra (in Uttar Pradesh), an area where tourism is high as well as along high-density transport routes.

Reports from the states—governments as well as NGOs—show that the focus of activities to date has been more on the rehabilitation of victims of trafficking than on combating or curbing trafficking networks.

However, even in these states some action has begun such as internal consultations on setting up inter-departmental committees to combat trafficking. Interestingly, only one state among those to report on the progress of actions against trafficking, has extended the terms of the action plan to cover trafficking for sexual exploitation as well as trafficking for exploitation of child labour.

Most reporting states have conducted field based surveys. And reports from most states are that corruption and gender-discriminatory attitudes are widely prevalent among law enforcement bodies, especially the police. Most states have also begun identifying NGOs with whom they can work in the initiatives against trafficking. A number of the pilot surveys have been supported by UNICEE.

NGOs are active in all states, and most are involved in efforts to help victims of trafficking to resettle and rehabilitate themselves. Some organisations are, however, equally focused on combating trafficking. Other national networks have been campaigning on policy and legal issues, as have some local NGOs.

Most NGOs are inclined towards strong community-based initiatives. While many in some of the southern states began organising against commercial sexual exploitation of children mainly through protests against the traditional *devdasi* or *jogin* systems, others began initiatives against exploitation of children by tourists. Others, many of them based in the metro centers, were drawn to putting the spotlight on trafficking because of their work among sex workers in so-called 'red light' areas.

NGOs working with child labour, or on health issue, were pulled into addressing issues of trafficking because of the frequently evident links between trafficking and commercial sexual abuse surfacing among the communities with which they were working.

Kerala: Action Against Traffickers

The state government is close to finalizing a plan for action against traffickers, following state-wide consultations with NGOs, law enforcement agencies and various government departments supported by international organisations such as UNICEF.

The State has recently conducted studies identifying the nature of sexual exploitation of children in urban areas and the methods of trafficking.

Kerala is the new tourist destination in India, having recently been designated one of the ten top "desirable" such destinations in the world by the International Tourism Organisation (ITO). It is also a source of very high levels of international migration from India.

Consequently, NGOs as well as the State Government have prioritised the need to focus on trafficking and commercial sexual abuse of children. The people's Council for Social Justice (PCSJ), a Kochi-based NGO that has been active for nearly 20 years in the area of legal advocacy, believes that communities need to be aware of the dangers of trafficking and alert to the modus operandi of traffickers. In addition to widespread awareness creation campaigns, PCSJ also conducts Lok Neethi Melas, people's courts, as which various problems are aired.

While some problems are settled, where possible, at the people's courts, others are referred to relevant government departments. The PCSJ works close with government.

Fighting Trafficking and Commercial Child Sexual Abuse

Inter-state co-operation has got underway with the directive to all State Government on formulating action plans against trafficking. Alongside, consultation if underway regarding the formation of a nodal agency to monitor trafficking, with representatives from Union and State Governments, inter-state law enforcement agencies, including officers of the police and judiciary, and NGOs.

Alongside, one of the most significant steps the government has taken is to direct that officials from the districts within each state—which are also extremely effective administrative units, numbering 466 in all—should send periodic reports of any activity related to trafficking as well as steps taken or planned to counter this.

More than so NGOs spread through the country work actively among sex workers: most have inevitably been drawn into confronting issues of trafficking. There are other addressing issues of trafficking of orphans, of children for labour, and yet others trafficking of migrants, including children. The Government works with all the organisations, the alliance varying in area of activity and degree of co-ordination, but in place, nevertheless, waiting to be tapped further. A fresh invitation has recently been issued by the DWCD, inviting submissions from NGOs, for proposals on actions that can serve to combat trafficking in children.

A recently begun endeavour to begin profiling of NGOs working with victims of trafficking is expected to make alliances more effective, as documentation of case studies and initiatives by these organisations would help identify resources for specific needs.

The SAARC Efforts Against Trafficking

From the SAARC Declarations

"The Heads of State or Government recalled that the Ninth SAARC Summit expressed concern at the trafficking of women and children within and between countries and pledged to co-ordinate efforts of Member states to take effective measures to address this problem. In this context, they welcomed the finalisation of the draft text on the Regional Convention on Combating the Crime of Trafficking in Women and Children for Prostitution and noted that this would be a vital instrument in dealing with this problem."

The Government of India works closely with UN agencies such as the UNICEF, UNIFEM and UNHCR, in its efforts to combat trafficking in children and other persons. India's National Plan for action on Child Trafficking was in fact drawn up principally by the Department of Women and Child Development. The review and implementation of the plan, numerous sensitisation programmes under it, development of documents and collation of information are also being jointly undertaken.

The Government also works with agencies such as the US Department of State and its department for legal enforcement, the USAID, the UK-based DFID, the Swedish and Canadian international development agencies, Dutch support oranisations and others in the campaign against trafficking.

With international support, the Indian Government, in alliance with NGOs, has developed and is conducting interactive training programmes to improve anti-trafficking co-ordination among law includes indepth instruction on recognising potential trafficking situations for border officers and other police personnel, and training for prosecutors in building successful prosecutions of traffickers and abettors.

The Government of India is also part of several regional and international initiatives. The focus of this effort is strengthening enforcement of existing laws, supporting NGOs shelters for victims of trafficking, and supporting rehabilitative programmes, including skills training and income generating activities.

India is the principal destination in the region for trafficking of children and other persons from Nepal, Bhutan and Bangladesh and as such has a critical role in curbing trafficking in the region. It has been part of regional monitoring efforts, such as the Asian Regional Initiative Against Trafficking in Women and Children (ARIAT).

The RESISTANCE movement against trafficking

RESISTANCE, a South Asian network of NGOs against trafficking was formed in 1996. One of its activities is to organise fact-finding missions to areas of heavy trafficking in women and children. Along with the Asian Women's Human Rights Commission (AWHRC) and the Global Alliance Against Traffic in Women (GAATW) it has conducted three such investigations, among these areas on the Indo-Myanmar border and the Bangladesh-India border.

Initiatives in Rehabilitation and Social Revolution: Fighting Trafficking and Commercial Child Sexual Abuse in Indias

"Stockholm commitment VII, VIII, IX, X; Agenda for Action II and III: Develop and implement gender-sensitive programmes, ensuring child participation; Set up safe havens for victims and adopt a non-punitive approach to victims, providing counselling and recovery and rehabilitation programmes as well as programmes for alternative means of livelihood; Create a social climate against trafficking and commercial sexual abuse of children, with focus on access to education (including education about child rights within the family); Mobilise political and other partners in this effort; Enhance the role of popular movements, Identify and strengthen civil society networks to combat trafficking.

Poverty is the pool from which traffickers catch their prey. Rooted in this belief, the Government of India's efforts to combat trafficking is three-pronged:

- Strengthen administrative and legal tools to battle traffickers;
- Help resettle victims of trafficking; and
- Develop economic fundamentals so that traffickers do not find easy prey.

Legal amendments, initiatives involving the police and judiciary and other administrative officials serve the first. This includes not just the law enforcement and monitoring efforts, but also endeavours to sensitise medical professionals and social workers, in addition to similar training programmes for police, judicial and other administrative officials.

Efforts at rehabilitating and resettling victims of trafficking and commercial sexual exploitations, while most are long-standing, are being reviewed. The changing view of victims is beginning to inform such activity as much as the amendments to the law– especially as NGOs become more vociferous in their criticism of moralising' and about the lack of volition or free choice to victims who are inmates at rehabilitation centres and shelters. The increasingly more sensitive approach also has government agencies initiating counselling facilities at these centers and stepping up skills training programmes for future income-generation.

Karnataka: Helping *Devdasis* to help themselves

The Government has initiated programmes to institute Self-help groups (SHOs) for *devdasis*, victims of the traditional form of sexual exploitation whereby young pre-adolescent girls were dedicated ("married") to the temple god and so became sexually available to the temple priests and other high-caste men of the community.

Launched in six districts of the state, the programmes offer development in skills such as making incense (*agarbatti*), tailoring and handloom weaving, and helping the former *devdasis* to secure alternate employment. The programme has also tied up with the Karnataka State Industrial Development Corporation (KSIDC) for marketing of the goods made by the beneficiaries.

Among the NGOs that work with this programme are the *Devdasi* Vimochana Punarvasti Sangh.

The Union Government runs 80 'rescue' homes for victims of such exploitation, in addition to which every district has a shelter for children who have been victimized. It has also recently initiated the Swadhar programme for resettlement of victims in close alliance with NGOs. One of the elements of this programme is a networking helpline between NGOs and government agencies, which can also help in monitoring trafficking activities.

The conditions at these centers have come under severe scrutiny from both NGOs and the media. While corrective steps are almost always taken immediately upon instances of such criticism, a system where such abuses do not take place can become effective only once the enforcement of laws becomes more effective.

NGOs have been the most effective at resettling victims of commercial sexual exploitation. From Sanlaap in West Bengal, to

Samskar in Andhra Pradesh, India Council for Child Welfare ((ICCW) in Tamil Nadu, Prayas, Snchalaya. Vanchit Vikas and Kehdi Vikas Mandal in Maharashtra, or Joint Women's Programme and Butterflies in Delhi, there is a host of organisations with dedicated workers helping to reintegrate victims of trafficking and commercial sexual exploitation and their vulnerable dependents in mainstream society. Many, like Odanadi in Karnataka, have actually confronted, or baded in ongoing efforts, traffickers to rescue victims.

NGOs have gone beyond 'rescue' to actually resettle victims. The Government has undoubtedly launched progammes and set up rescue home, out the NGOs have helped take the victims out of the programmes and homes and help reintegrated them in society. Some like the psychiatry department at the National Institute of Mental Health and Neuro Sciences (NIMHANS) specialize in counselling, though most provide some services to help the reintegration process on the victim's part.

Andhra Pradesh: 'Rescue' Policy soon; fighting the *jogin* tradition

The State Government is close to finanlising a 'rescue' policy for child victims of trafficking. The Recent (October 2001) scandal over a prominent medical practioner in Hyderabad, the Andhra Pradesh Capital, being accused of trafficking in babies for adoption, has inspired urgency in ongoing state-level inter-departmental consultations regarding modalities to combat traffickers. Particular emphasis is being given to law enforcement.

The drought-prone areas of the state yield large bodies of migrants, always a rich source for trafficking networks. In addition, the state is reported to have poor law enforcement as well several reported cases of genuer-insensitive police harassment.

Initiatives with NGOs are ongoing, principally in a community-based programme for children invulnerable situations, including children of sex workers in Anantapur district as well as similar projects under the Prajwala and Abhaya trusts. The Government has also begun a survey of the extent of the practice of the jogin tradition, dedicating children to temple gods for sexual prostitution subsequently.

Samskar, an NGO in Nizamabad district, has been working for close to 20 years to fight the jogin Tradition. In over 400 villages of the district, it has helped educate and train children of jogins in skills to provide an alternate means of livelihood, in the process breaking the vicious circle of exploitation.

Among the NGOs working with child sex workers, is the Vasavya Mahila Mandal (VMM), which works to combat trafficking mainly through mobilizing support from existing community networks. VMM has rallied the support of women's committees in at least 50 communities of Krishna district, and, with funding support from the DWCD, Government of India, has trained and helped resettle child victims of trafficking.

It is equally true that NGOs have made government-launched economic help programmes such as the Rashtriya Mahila Kosh or the Mahila Samriddhi Yojana effective.

None of the initiatives against trafficking would be meaningful without social acceptance of these. Neither in the law enforcement against traffickers, nor in the efforts to help victims of trafficking find a new life, would any government or NGO effort work if the community does not participate by supporting these efforts.

Madhya Pradesh: Jabali for Children

The decade-old government scheme works with voluntary organisations in the attempt to "eliminate commercial sexual exploitation" in the state. Focusing particularly on children in certain castes and tribes where trafficking and such exploitation is more common, Jabali (literally meaning 'Our children') not only provides temporary shelter for victims, it also provides health are and training in skills that can provide alternate sources of income.

Bihar & Jharkhand: NGO Initiatives Prevail

While the State Governments are engaged yet in preliminary research and documentation, NGO initiatives against trafficking of children for commercial sexual abuse have mushroomed in both Bihar and Jharkhand.

Using theatre as an effective medium of communications in what is a predominantly an illiterate populace, beginning in Katihar and Purnea districts, NGOs have been effectively monitoring cases of child sexual abuse, commercial and otherwise. A poster campaign is also underway, mainly addressing children.

State-wide networks in Bihar and Jharkhand, linked to the national body Action Against Trafficking and Sexual Exploitation of Children (ATSEC), work closely with the police and the state departments of welfare. Consequently, instances of sexual abuse of children, both commercial and within homes, is being more frequently reported. As a field worker said, "The lid is cracking."

NGOs have been particularly focused on drawing communities into the fight against trafficking, perhaps this being the most onerous aspect of that battle.

Sex workers view outsiders with suspicion. NGO workers, consequent to dedicated work over decades, find their interventions more readily accepted by victims of trafficking than officialdom.

Rehabilitation efforts by the Government are generally 'top-down'. This is about to change. The Government proposes to invite voices representing children and to that end is currently working on setting up a Commission for Children and putting in place a National Policy on Child Rights as well as a proposed Charter for Children.

These will help implement the government's commitment to "Children's right to survival, health and nutrition, play and leisure, early childhood care and education,... life and liberty, name and nationality, the right to a family and the right to be protected from exploitation" as stated in the Convention on the Rights of the Child.

The commitment focuses on the special needs of children form marginalised and disadvantaged communities, which is the source for trafficking, and child victims of all forms of abuse, particularly for sex and pornography.

The Government of India has recently launched a scheme called Ballika Samriddhi Yojana with the objective to change the negative family and community attitudes towards the girl child, to improve enrolment and retention of girl children in schools, to raise the age of marriage, to assist the girl undertake income generating activities. The scheme covers girl children of families below the poverty line as defined by the Government of India. Under this scheme, the eligible girl children are entitled a past birth grant amount of Rupees 500 and annual scholarship ranging from Rupees 300 per annum to Rupees 1000 per annum for classes 1 to 10.

How effectively this programme will be implemented undoubtedly will be decided civil society, but it is the government that has taken the first step in what may well become a measure that will curb not only trafficking, but also female foeticide and infanticide, child marriage, and ensure better nutrition for the girl child.

The issues oi trafficking and the commercial sexual exploitation of women and children or "prostitution" as it is commonly called are gaining prominence in international circles, among NGOs, Governments and concerned citizens. Prostitution has been called "the oldest oppression by the National Commission for Women. In different times in history it has been tolerated, encouraged, prohibited and regulated. In recent times the issue has come centre stage because of:

(a) increasing reports of commercial sexual exploitation of children,

(b) the scare of women and children in prostitution being carriers of AIDS/HIV while the exploiter who has infected the women or child is forgotten.

(c) greater awareness and emphasis on rights of children,

(d) the global movement for redefining gender relations of subordination and for gender justice,

(e) structural adjustment policies in developing countries which have in many cases led to growing number of female headed households and the feminisation of poverty.

(f) growth of sex tourism, the entertainment industry, pornography in print, electronic and cyber media.

(g) changing public attitudes towards sex and morality.

(h) the economic and law and order ramfications of trafficking and commercial sexual exploitation which are part of the huge global narcoterrorist criminal network.

(i) women victims of commercial sexual exploitation organising themselves to access their rights and

(j) weakening of the family structure, changing social and family scenario.

It is in this background that this report seeks to examine the issue of trafficking and commercial sexual exploitation of women and child in the country. In order to place this in the right perspective, a presentation of a short summary of the various aspects of this phenomenon is in order.

Various terms are used while speaking of this subject like prostitute, women and children in prostitution, commercial sex workers, sex worker etc. The words "prostitution" and "prostitute" have derogatory connotations wherein the stigma of the offence is placed on the victim. It is therefore proposed to use the term" commercial sexual exploitation of women and children" which was also used in the Declaration of the World Congress against Commercial Sexual Exploitation of Children.

"Child" has been defined in the Convention on the Rights of the child ratified by India, as a person below 18 years of age. The definition differs in various legislations in India from 12 years in the Indian Penal Code (IPC) to 18 years for a female child in the Child Marriage Restraint Act. However, in the Immoral Traffic (Prevention) Act, 1956 (ITPA) the term child refers to a person who has not completed the age of sixteen years. A minor means a person who has completed the age of 16 years but has not completed the age of 18 years. Both the child and the minor are given special protection under Section 6-2 (a) of the ITPA. The Child marriage Restraint Act has fixed the age of 18 years keeping in view the girl child which renders sexual relation and pregnancy harmful and even life threatening to her below that age. From this perspective the sexually exploited child is more at risk, being forced into multiple sexual relations. Hence, we may use the more widely accepted definition of child as being below 18 years of age for the purpose of definition commercial sexual exploitation of the child or children of women victims.

It has been pointed out that many states refuse to recognise the problem of commercial sexual exploitation of children because of a misconception of the definition of the age of a child. This situation needs to be rectified by creating greater awareness of the meaning of the term-commercial sexual exploitation of children.

Modes of Initiation into Commercial Sexual Exploitation

The causes of commercial sexual exploitation of women and children are many. Initiation into commercial sexual exploitation is through different routes. Firstly children and women are inducted forcibly through abduction, trafficking and deceit. Secondly there are children of women victims who are inducted into the racket by pimps/brothel keepers an sometimes even by the mother herself. Thirdly, caste and tribal sanctions/practices of certain castes and tribes like Nats/Raj Nats, who were traditional performers in Uttar Pradesh (UP) and Rajasthan; Bedias of UP, Rajasthan and Madhya Pradesh (M.P.); Bhartu and Habura who were so-called criminal communities in U.P.: Dehredar of former singers and dancer in U.P. Gandharvas or singers in U.P Kanjars – a wandering community in M.P., Rajasthan and U.P. is another route. The loss of traditional means of livelihood due to the spread of modern forms of entertainment forces many in these communities to allow the exploitation of their girls/women. Fourthly, the religious practice of dedication of girls in the name of God as in the Devadasi, Jogin, Basavi, Venkataani, Practices which, though banned in the states of Karnataka, Maharashtra, Andhra Pradesh, though banned in the states of Karnataka. Maharashtra, Andhra Pradesh, Tamil Nadu and Goa where they were previously practiced, continued on a lower scale in a clandestine manner in some of thee states. Fifthly, women who are in economic distress due to lack of means of livelihood, widowhood separation by husbands, abandonment by family etc., are, much against their choice, forced to become victims of commercial sexual exploitation. Sixthly, migrant women from within the country or from neighouring counties are more likely to be forced to become victims. Seventhly, girls in the fringes of the entertainment industry. Such as bar girls, cabaret dancers etc. are also vulnerable.

Though there are a number of studies and reports on commercial sexual exploitation of women and children there are no reliable estimates of the extent and magnitude of trafficking and commercial sexual exploitation in India. There are major obstacles in trying to estimate the magnitude of the problem, among which are the social stigma and legal sanctions attached to it which inhibit easy identification, the stranglehold of gangs and brothel keepers enforced through violence which prevents identification of the women and child victims and the dispersed nature of the phenomenon, other than in certain localities of the metropolitan cities.

A survey sponsored by the Central Social Welfare Board (CSWB) in 1991 in six metropolitan cities of India indicated that the population of women and child victims of commercial sexual exploitation would be between 70,000 to 1,00,000. It also revealed that about 30 per cent of them are below 18 years of age. Nearly 40 per cent of them were inducted when they were less than 18 years of age. The major contributory factor for the commercial sexual exploitation of women and children are poverty and unemployment or lack of appropriate rehabilitation. 70 per cent of them are illiterates. 43 per cent of them desire to be rescued. Most of those who want to leave have given the reasons of desire to save their children from commercial sexual exploitation and protection of the future of their children, fear of disease etc. the others continue to be exploited due to absence of alternative sources of income, social non-acceptability, family customs, poverty, ill health and their despondence.

Commercial sexual exploitations is found in a concentrated manner in brothels and red light areas. The more dispersed form may be found along major highways, in massage parlours, guest house, call girl rackets, cabaret shows, female escort services etc.

Situation of Women and Child Victims of Commercial Sexual Exploitation

Trafficking and commercial sexual exploitation of women and children is a fundamental violation of the rights of women and children. The social, physical, psychological and moral consequences of commercial sexual exploitation on women and child victims are serious, life-long and even life threatening. About 60-80 per cent of the victims suffer from more than one disease. Threat of unwanted pregnancy, maternity mortality, torture, physical injury, physical disabilities, mental traumas and disorders and sexually transmitted diseases including HIV/AIDS is ever present.

The life of a woman or child victim of commercial sexual exploitation is under constant fear of the police, of the primps, of brothel keepers etc., The children of women victims are born and are brought up with the stigma of illegitimacy. Shunned by the majority, they are in danger of being caught up in the grip of various vices and criminal activities. They also develop a fatalistic attitude which makes rehabilitation difficult.

Most women are daughters who out of a strong feeling of filial piety maintain their parents, dependents per cent even the families of husbands, lovers, pimps etc. with what is left of their income. Most women also have children who are solely dependent on them. according to the survey by the CSWB about 60% belong to the Scheduled Castes and Scheduled Tribes (SCs/STs) and the Other Backward Classes. The large majority are Hindus.

At the macro level, the women and child victims are in a very helpless condition, caught up in the strangle hold of organised criminal networks with enormous economic turnover involving a variety of operators staring form pimps, house owners, broth keepers, taxi drivers, hotel managements, industrial interests and the local police.

Legal Framework

The Right against exploitation is a fundamental right guaranteed by the Constitution of India. Under Article 23, traffic in human beings, "beggar" and other similar forms of forced labour are prohibited and any contravention of this provision shall be an offence punishable in accordance with the law.

The Immoral Traffic (Prevention) Act, 1956 (ITPA) supplemented by the Indian Penal Code (IPC) prohibits trafficking in human beings including children and lays down severe penalties. The ITPA and IPC prescribe punishment for crimes related to prostitution. The ITPA covers offences of exploitation of both girls and boys. One special feature of the Act as amended is, that the presumption of guilt Is laid on the accused in cases where children or minors are found in a brothel and on medical examination are detected to have been sexually abused. The ITPA contains enhanced punishments for offences in respect of a child or a minor.

Under Section 5 of the ITP Act procuring, inducing or taking a child or a minor for the sake of prostitution is punishable with rigorous imprisonment for a term of not less than 7 years but which may extend even to life. Under Section 6 where a child is found with a person in a brothel, there is a presumption of guilt for detaining the child on the person and he shall be punishable with imprisonment. Under Section 7 where a person commits the offence of prostitution in respect of a child or minor, he shall be punishable with imprisonment for not less than 7 years or for life, for a term which may extend to 10 years and fine.

The incidence reported Under Immoral Traffic (Prevention) Act continued to show a declining trend. It has a desirable fall of 16.6 per cent in 1995 compared to the previous year. The States of Tamil Nadu (5110), Karnataka (1851), Maharashtra (560), Andhra Pradesh (507 and National Capital Territory of Delhi (125) have been enforcing this Act with considerable effort compared to other States/Union Territories (UTs). The above 5 states registered almost 96.5 per cent of the total cases reported in the country in

1995. The law enforcement agencies of the above States/UTs found enforcement of this special Act as vital and the cases were registered as preventive drive in containing the social evil. In contrast, the other States/UTs hardly enforced this Acts as revealed from the number of cases registered by them. This aspect is revealed in the publication Crime in India-1995 published by Ministry of Home Affairs, Government of India.

The Juvenile Justice Act, 1986 provides for the care, protection, treatment and rehabilitation of neglected or delinquent juveniles including girls. The enforcement of the ITPA, IPC and the Juvenile Justice Act is the responsibility of the State Government.

Section 13(4) of the ITPA provides that the Central Government appoint such number of police officers as trafficking police officers and they shall exercise such powers and discharge such functions in relation to the whole of India. The matter was taken up with Central Bureau of Investigation. They have expressed willingness to play a role in cases where organised gangs of persons are perpetuating this crime across national and international borders thought in a limited number of cases having grave ramifications.

A review of the Immoral Traffic Prevention Act is also underway. For this purpose the National Law School University of India was entrusted with the task of reviewing the Act and proposing amendments/new legislation to make it more effective and stringent. The National Law School, University of India has submitted its report. In the Report they have proposed two different draft Bills containing different policies and legal arrangements to deal with the problems.

The first draft Bill is the prevention of Immoral Traffic and the Rehabilitation of Prostituted Persons Bill, 1993. This is a Bill to prohibit immoral trafficking in women and children and to mitigate the sufferings of victims of prostitution. The second Draft Bill is entitled, "The Prohibition of Immoral Traffic and Empowerment of Sexual Workers Bill, 1993." This is a Bill to prohibit immoral trafficking especially in women and children and to confer rights on sexual workers with a view to prevent sexual exploitation and protect health and hygiene in sexual work. Both these Bills have bee referred to the National Commission for Women (NCW) for obtaining their comments.

Orders by the Supreme Court of India

The Supreme Court of India has passed tow important judgments on the subject of commercial sexual exploitation of children and women and the rescue and rehabilitation of children of women victims.

On the specific problem of child prostitution, in a public interest litigation, Vishal Jeet vs. Union of India, the Supreme Court of India passed an order on 2.5.1990, after hearing various parties on the subject of "child Prostitution" which stated that the Central and State Government should set up Advisory Committees to make suggestions for:

(a) the measure to be taken in eradicating child prostitution.

(b) the social welfare programmes to be implemented for the care, protection, treatment, development and rehabilitation of the young fallen victims and mainly children and girls rescued either from the brothel houses or from the vice of prostitution.

(c) to make suggestions of amendments of the existing laws or for enactment of an new law if so warranted for the prevention of sexual exploitation of children.

(d) the examination of the Devdasi and Jogin traditions and give suggestions for their welfare and rehabilitation.

(e) devising suitable machinery for implementing the suggestions made by the Committee.

The Supreme Court gave these direction to the Union of India and all States and Union Territories in the country. These were also communicated by the Union Government to all States and Union Territories for taking appropriate action in accordance with the Court order.

In pursuance of the court directives, the Government of India constituted a Central Advisory Committee on Child Prostitution. The recommendations made by the Central Advisory Committee have been sent to the concerned Central Ministries/Departments and to the State Governments/UT Administrations for taking appropriate action. To implement the recommendations of the Central Advisory Committee, a Desk has been set up in the Department of Women and Child Development, Ministry of Human Resource Development, Government of India.

State Governments have also set up State Advisory Committees and are taking action to notify special police officers, set up Advisory Boards of Social Workers and NGOs in red light areas, conduct regular raids and take measures for the protection and rehabilitation of rescued persons.

In the second case of Gaurav Jain *vs.* Union of India the Supreme Court passed an order dated 9th July, 1997 directing, interalia, the constituting of a committee to make an indepth study of the problems of prostitution, child prostitutes and to evolve suitable schemes to their rescue and rehabilitation.

As directed by the Supreme Court the Committee on Prostitution, child prostitutes and children of prostitutes (see Annexure-I) headed by Secretary, Department of Women and Child Development has made an in-depth study into the problems of commercial sexual exploitation and trafficking of women and children and of children of the women victims, to evolve such suitable schemes as are appropriate and consistent with the directions given by the Supreme Court. Secretary, Department of Women and Child Development, the Chairperson of the Committee and the Member-Secretary of the Committee, Visited Bombay, Bhopal and Chennai. Meetings and discussions were held with officers of the State Governments in charge of Women and Child Development, law enforcement, social defence, legislative, matters, SC/ST welfare and with NGOs working for the rescue and reintegration of women and child victims of commercial sexual exploitation and children of women victims, experts and social workers. Projects in red light areas and high supply areas were also visited. Documents on the strategies adopted in other countries were studied. The study report of the CSWB, the report on the Regional consultations held by the Department and UNICEF, the reports of the NCW on the subject and the report of the Central Advisory Committee on eradication of child prostitution, its findings and recommendations and other reports were also studied.

CHAPTER 6

Rehabilitation of Women and Child Victims—Intervention of NGOs

The Central Social Welfare Board provides financial assistance to NGOs to run Development and Care Centres for the children of victims of prostitution. These centers are set up in red light areas and provide facilities of crèche and day-care centre, educational support programme, supplementary nutrition, health care, counselling, excursions etc. and are manned by trained Social Workers and trained teachers. The ministry of Welfare also provides financial assistance to NGOs for the rehabilitation of children of prostitutes. The number of such protective homes is estimated to be about 80. Protective Homes provide custodial care and protection in addition to providing education and Vocational training and arranging measures in rehabilitation of the inmates. However, there are many inadequacies in the running of these Homes. The Government also has an extensive network of Short Stay Homes assisted by the DWCD and Juvenile Homes set up under the Juvenile Justice Act for protection and rehabilitation of the victims. The services of qualified doctors and psychiatrists are available in the Short Stay Homes. These services are available on part time basis in the Homes under Juvenile Justice Act.

In some red light areas, projects have been sanctioned by the

Government of India for starting centers under the Integrated Child Development Services Scheme (ICDS). However, the response from NGOs in starting these sanctioned centers is not encouraging. A number of voluntary agencies are also independently involved in the care and rehabilitation of women victims, including child victims and advocacy of their problems. Projects for rehabilitation of *Devadasis, Jogins,* women victims etc., are also taken up under various schemes for training and employment of women like Support for Training and Employment Programme (STEP), (Setting up of Training cum Employment cum Production Units (NORAD) and by Shramik Vidyapeeths assisted by the Central Government.

A National Plan of Action for the SAARC Decade (1991-2000) of the Girl Child focusing on the survival, protection and development of the girl child has been formulated. A special set of interventions for adolescent girls has been institutionalised through the ICDS infrastructure. Programmes of action and advocacy are being implemented to project positive images of girl children so as to bring about changes in societal attitudes towards them.

Since the incidence of prostitution is also related to the low status of women in society, Government is implementing various programmes of: (a) Training-cum-Income Generating activities such as NORAD, STEP, CCEVT, SEP, DWCRA, to economically empower women. A 40 per cent reservation for women has been provided under the Integrated Rural Development Programme (IRDP). (b) As a special measure of affirmative action, the Rashtriya Mahila Kosh has been set up to provide micro-credit to poor women in the informal sector with low transaction cost through the mediation of NGOs. The Mahila Samridhi Yojana has been introduced to enable women to exercise greater control over household savings. (c) Support services such as Working Women Hostels, Short Stay Homes, Creches, family counselling centers etc. (d) Awareness Generation Programmes for Women and dissemination regarding their rights.

Further to formulate policy guidelines and a programme

document to support future NGO/ Pilot projects and strategies for developing a data base on the magnitude and dimensions of the problem of child prostitution, this Department and UNICEF held 6 regional workshops covering all States and UTs at Bangalore, Goa, Hyderabad, Patna, Chandigarh and Calcutta in 1996.

The National Human Rights Commission (NHRC) has also constituted a core group to study the problem of child prostitution in Delhi and Karnataka and to work out preventive and rehabilitative strategis.

State Government Initiatives

State Government have been implementing a number of projects for the rescue and rehabilitation of women and children victims through their own agencies and in collaboration with NGOs.

The Devadasi rehabilitation scheme of the Karnataka Government a consists of four components. It is being implemented in 6 districts of the State. Self help groups of devadasis have also been formed.

First, training in skill development is offered through courses in different vocations like handloom weaving, agarbathi making, tailoring etc, to able bodies Devadasis in the age group of 18-25 years. This was subsequently linked up with marketing centers after the formation of Industrial Co-operative Units in various trades.

The second component, imparting of social and moral education was necessary for the moral and social upliftment of Devadasis alongwith their economic rehabilitation.

The other components were for the health care of *Devadasis* with emphasis on research and co-operation and provision for Seminars/Workshops to disseminate experience. Residential schools to admit children of *Devadasis* and also other children have been set up in the districts where this practice was prevalent.

Government of Andhra Pradesh has sanctioned a project in 1997-98 for rehabilitation of women victims of commercial sexual exploitation who are HIV infected. Surveys have been conducted or initiated in a few states.

Government of Maharashtra has set up special Juvenile Homes with facilities of counselling, vocational training and health unit for children affected by commercial sexual exploitation and HIV/AIDS. Maintenance grant of Rs. 300/- p.m. is given to *Devadasis* and their children are supplied with free educational material.

The Government of Madhya Pradesh has stared a Scheme called Jabali in 1992-93. the objective of this scheme is to assist Voluntary Organisations to take up activities for the welfare and development of women and child victims of commercial sexual exploitation so as to eliminate commercial sexual exploitation. The Scheme is mainly targeted at the women and children in those caste/tribes where there is social acceptance and even collusion by the male members with the commercial sexual exploitation of their women. The scheme has five components:

1. Running of Boarding Schools for children or women victims.
2. Setting up protective homes for young girls.
3. Providing women victims with benefits for income generation and economic rehabilitation.
4. Creation of public awareness through information, education and publicity.
5. Health checkups and treatment.

This Scheme is an integrated, well designed scheme. However it is reported that all components of the scheme are not being implemented.

A number of NGOs are working for the welfare of women & child victims like Bharatiya Patita Uddhar Sangh (Delhi), Prerana (Bombay), Joint Women's Programme, Devadasi Vimochan Punarvasti Sangh (Belgaum), Satya Shodhyan Ashram (Madhya Pradesh), Gram Niyojan Kendra (U.P.) Sanlaap (West Bengal) etc. For instance the Shrimant Dagadee Seth Halwai Ganapathi Trust, Pune provides institutional services to children through its 3 Bal Sangopan Centres based on the cottage system. Prerana of Bombay has been organising services for institutional care of children, providing night shelter, balwadi, educational support programme, women's empowerment programmes in the red light areas of Bombay. Vanchit Vikas and Devadasi Niradhar Mukti Kendra, Gandhigan are two other NGO's Working in Pune. A list of agencies and individuals who are working among women and child victims or are interested in their problems is at Annexure-II (Source: Girl Child Prostitution in India – Dr. K.K. Kukherjee).

State Governments have also been tackling this problem by organising raids to detect commercial sexual exploitation, especially of children, and to rescue the victims. A major raid was organized in Mumbai ion 5th February 1996 wherein 484 victims including more than 2000 girls from Nepal were rescued. Most of them were sent back to their homes or to rehabilitation centers in other states. This is reported to have had a positive impact in acting as a detergent of brothel keepers, pimps etc. atleast to control commercial sexual exploitation of children.

Issue of Commercial Sexual Exploitation

Inspite of many interventions for prevention, law enforcement, rescue and rehabilitation, there does not appear to have been much impact on the prevealence of commercial sexual exploitation of women and child except in the case of the Devadasi system which has nearly been eliminated in the States where it existed.

The reasons for this include:

(a) Lack of seriousness among law enforcement machinery and administration in addressing this problem due to, among other reasons, ambivalent attitude of society to the problem of commercial sexual exploitation as such;

(b) Risks, including threat to life an property, faced by social workers, NGO's and Government officials who are sincerely working for the welfare of women and child victims and the consequent unwillingness of other Ngo's and officials to work in red light area and among victims;

(c) Insufficient awareness about the prevalence and remifications of child trafficking could be one reasons for lack of strong action;

(d) Lure of comfortable life style for victims compared to work burden and poverty at home. This makes it more difficult to persuade some victims to come out of the profession and be rehabilitated especially when they would earn less in another trade;

(e) Social stigma and family problems faced by victims as a result of which they are either not willing to return to their families and/or their families are not willing to accept the;

(f) Difficulties in estimation the age of child victims;

(g) Insufficient infrastructure in the form of institutions for stay and rehabilitation of rescued victims. Reluctance of certain institutions and NGO's to house and care for rescued victims due to social stigma attached to them.

(h) Lack of co-ordination between border police forces of neighbouring countries to stop inter country trafficking.

(i) Lack of support lines, drop-in centers for women to seek comfort when they are mentally traumatized.

A number of recommendation on combating trafficking and commercial sexual exploitation of women and child have been made in various reports, studies, national and international conferences. The Report of the Central Advisory Committee on Child Prostitution, the recommendation of the National Commission for Women and the direction of the supreme Court of India and the experiences of various NGO's working in this area are very relevant. In order that these recommendations are property disseminated and acted upon it is necessary to have a comprehensive Plan of Action to combat trafficking and the commercial sexual exploitation of women and child. This would guide the actions of the Ministries/Departments of the Central Government the state Governments, NGO's the public and private sector ad other Sections of civil society. The Draft Plan of Action outlined below consist of action point grouped under:

1. Prevention

2. Trafficking
3. Awareness Generation and Social Mobilisation
4. Health Care Services
5. Education and child Care
6. Housing, Shelter and Civic Amenities
7. Economic Empowerment
8. Legal Reforms and Law Enforcement
9. Rescue and Rehâbilitation
10. Institutional Machinery
11. Methodology

The ultimate objective of this Plan of Action is to main stream and to reintegrate women and child victims of commercial sexual exploitation in society. Therefore, the provision of services or implementation of measures listed in this Plan of Action are only temporary interventions for the interregnum. Specialised services would be provided only to enable them to access existing schemes and services on par with other citizens.

Prevention

1. High supply areas of women and child victims, the trafficking routes and mechanisms have been identified in some reports. Details of districts and even villages have been documented. The Central and State Governments will take up long-term training-cum-income generation projects under IRDP, Development of Women and Children in Rural Areas, CAPART Schemes, Khadi and Village Industries Commission Schemes, STEP, Socio-Economic Programme, NORAD, Rashtriya Mahila Kosh, Prime Minister Rozgar Yojana, Swarna Jayanti Shahri Rozgar Yojana, and other such existing schemes of the Government of India alongwith the schemes of State Governments in identified areas on priority. Wherever necessary, projects may be sanctioned under these schemes for benefiting families in which women or children are vulnerable to or at high risk of being trafficked and sexually exploited for

commercial purposes. NGOs working in the area will be involved.

2. Assisting and sponsoring studies to create a reliable and relevant data base on the high supply areas, routes, destinations, causes of commercial sexual exploitation, high risk groups, the exploiters, the magnitude of the problem etc.

3. Though universalisation of primary and elementary education is a macro level objective it is specially relevant to prevent girls and women, 70 per cent or more of whom are illiterate, from becoming victims of commercial sexual exploitation. Hence in selection of areas for projects and programmes for universalisation of access, participation and achievement in elementary education, the districts and areas within districts which are high supply areas should be given higher priority.

4. Setting up of Family Counseling Centres and Short Stay Homes in high supply areas to provide counselling and guidance to single women, which is a high risk group, who are deserted, widowed, divorced, socially ostracised, to parents of missing girls, illegally adopted girls, street children, child brides, bonded labourers etc., so that they get shelter and counselling.

5. Creating a safe and secure environment for women and children in society through:

(a) Formation of Committees for the Protection of Rights of women and children at District level, block level and Mohalla level/Village level/Panchayat at level with membership of the public. These committees may be vested with the function of monitoring the registration and investigation of crimes against women, expediting the measures for the defence of the rights of women and children, providing assistance to women for legal-aid and/or assisting women to defind themselves against criminal proceedings.

(b) Formation of Watchdog Committees. Community Surveillance Group, Neighbourhood Policing for mobilising all sections of society to counter crime against girls and women. Students and youths in neighbourthood and campuses to take responsibility for safety of girls students in the campus, prevent violation of women rights within the campus and protect and defend victims of such violation.

(c) Village Sakshrata Samities, Neighbourhood Development Committees, community Development Societies, Gram Mahila Mandals, Balika Mandals, Yuvak Mandals and the Gram Panchayats may be mobilised and activised to provide support services or assistance for the care and protection of women and children.

6. Co-ordination would be ensured among the Department of tourism, Border Police, Travel and tour operators, hotel managements, immigration officials to check the entry of convicted child sexual exploiters and sex tourists.

7. The local administration in the high areas of supply and red light areas where brothels are located would be made responsible for ensuring the safety and security of victims by taking speedy and effective action on reports about trafficking and commercial sexual exploitation. Heads of Schools, of institutions and of work places would be made sware of the risk of trafficking and their services enlisted to prevent such occurrence in their institution/work place.

8. Migrant girls and women in search of employment, who have run away or are driven away from their homes or those who are lost, are in danger of falling prey to commercial sexual exploitation. Contact centers will be established in major cities near railway stations and bus stations to give guidance and information to women in need of temporary shelter, about addresses of short stay homes, reception centres, shelter homes etc.

9. Self-defence training will be given as part of physical education to girl students, to enable them to develop self- confidence and defend themselves from being harassed, trafficked or exploited.

Trafficking

1. Establishment of a nodal agency to be set upon the lines of the Narcotics Bureau to stop trafficking in women and children will be seriously considered.

2. Appointment of trafficking police officers would be done to strictly enforce laws regarding prohibition of human trafficking.

3. Support would be given to establish a regional convention to combat the trafficking of women and children in prostitution, in SAARC region.

4. Strict instructions would be issued to immigration officers, Border Police authorities and local police in the transit, areas for the purpose of keeping a vigil on the entry of young girls under suspicious or unexplained circumstances into the country from neighouring countries.

5. Most of the human trafficking is done within the country from one State or region to another. To prevent this, assistance would be provided to NGO's to set up helplines. Help booths in identified bus and railway stations which are known transit points. Police, railway police and transport authorities would ensure surprise checking and inspection of persons taking young girls and women under suspicious circumstances for the purposes of trafficking in buses and trains and in bus and railway stations.

6. NGO's would be assisted to set up short Stay Homes near border posts on identified trafficking routes form neighbouring countries, to provide temporary shelter, care and counselling to women and children rescued from traffickers.

7. Indian Missions in important source countries would network with Ministry of Home Affairs and the Central Prevention and Rehabilitation Committee and helps; identifying areas from where there have been reports of organised trafficking to India so that movement of women and children across the border from these areas could be monitored return and rehabilitation of rescued women and children and preventive measures, if any, with the consent and co-operation of the country concerned. Comprehen-

sive guidelines will be formulated for dealing with the return and rehabilitation of women children of foreign origin. At the same time, Missions in demand countries (for child sex-tourism) would be asked to exercise greater vigil in issuing visas for convicted or suspected child abusers.

8. India will actively co-operate with the international community to combat trafficking and sexual exploitation of women and children.

Awareness Generation and Social Mobilisation

1. The public perception of women and child victims of commercial sexual exploitation is conditioned by patriarchal attitudes and gender roles. Hence myths about women willingly taking up this so called profession, about exploitation providing them a livelihood, about the need for providing "Safety valves" to ensure harmony and such like are touted and believed in. There is also an attitude of refusal to recognise the existence of trafficking and the commercial sexual exploitation of children. Such perceptions among the pubic need to be countered through removing gender bias in text books, teaching methods and media messages. Media campaigns that initiate a process of questioning gender roles, gender determination and project positive images of partnership between women and men, and of girl children and women be taken up. Such campaigns should be linguistically and culturally acceptable. Spots for TV, AIR and print media in national, regional and local languages may be prepared. Provision of funds be also made for broadcasting and telecasting of such spots, as most often awareness is not adequate due to lack of resources.

2. Training and programmes for activities for Youth organisations and local bodies should include a strong component of gender sensitisation and the role of gender in daily life.

3. Programmes of advocacy and information through the media, awareness generation camps, education work etc. would also sensitise citizens to the plight of women and child victims and the need to change social attitudes of stigmatising them and their

children.

4. Special modules of sensitisation for probation officers, personnel manning homes, police officials, judicial officers, border police, health personnel and NGO's towards the causes of commercial sexual exploitation and the situation of women and child victims would be prepared and used for training and orientation. Institutions like the National Institute of Social Defence and the proposed National and State Resource Centres for Women would be utilised for this purposes.

5. The Press Council of India and the broadcast media would be requested to adopt and strictly implement a code of conduct that protects the women/child victim's right to anonymity and privacy, since these two factors are critical for their survival. Publishing of photographs naming women arrested etc. should not be done except with their written consent. Media should also highlight the exploited and victimised state of women and child victims; the fact that they have themselves become victims of AIDS due to contact with an infected male person and their role in the prevention of HIV infection.

6. Programmes for spreading legal literacy would be given greater assistance by Central and State Governments and legal literacy components would be incorporated in all projects for human resource development and poverty alleviation in rural and urban areas.

7. Publicity campaigns targeted at potential victims and clients in urban areas and at parents, guardians, local authorities in high supply areas should be taken upto make them aware of the correct situation of victims of commercial sexual exploitation and the risks involved and to dispel prevailing myths abut sexual relations especially with children.

8. Programmes of providing education and knowledge about sex and reproduction must be implemented at an appropriate level in schools to dispel ignorance and thereby reduce the risk of deception of young girls for sexual abuse & commercial sexual exploitation. For non-school going youth specific programmes

may be implemented through Nehru Yuvak Kendras, non-formal education and other literacy centers etc.

9. In orders to raise the consciousness of the public and highlight the trafficking both of women and children, cases of conviction of exploiters, traffickers etc., will be given due publicity.

Health Care Services

1. While total elimination of commercial sexual exploitation of women and children is the objective, the fact that it continues to exist and would continue to exist in whatever magnitude or form, inspite of policies against it, cannot be ignored. Therefore, provision of health services of immediate nature which would mitigate the suffering of the victims and enable them to access their entitlement to their rights and Government services, in the primary health units or by NGO's, on par with other citizens, would be worked out.

2. Health cards to be issued to women and child victims ensuring free medical treatment, provision of adequate drugs and medications in Government institutions.

3. Health Cards Centres be set up, in or near red light areas, which would provide immunisation, primary health care, first aid, health Tuberculosis/HIV/AIDS education, gynaecological care facilities, free contraception and counseling. The timings of these centers should be convenient to the women and child victims. These could be set up by State Government or by NGO's with assistance from Central/State Governments.

4. Educational campaigns through various media about the risks of unprotected sex should be intensively done in known red light areas, on highways, and other identified centers where commercial sexual exploitation takes place.

5. Unethical, illegal and uninformed medical testing of women and child victims for HIV/AIDS/STD etc., which tends to violate their rights would not be done.

6. Psychological health of the women and child victims as well as children of the women victims is endangered use to the circumstances of their exploitation. Psychological counselling services should be provided on a part time basis in the health care centers. This could be done under the Family Counselling Centres Scheme of CSWB with specially trained counsellors.

7. Women victims suffering from terminal stages of AIDS would require separate shelter homes to be set up in major cities. NGO's and charitable organisations would be assisted by the National Aids Control Organisation to set up such homes.

Education and Child Care

1. Coercion to remove the child from the mother, wherever possible, would be more relevant in the context of the type of environment she lives in, for instance, in areas where brothels are located. Considering the fact that taking away a child from her mother by coercion would only add to her trauma and that of the mother and keeping in view the inadequacy of institutional facilities for sheltering the children, as far as possible, persuasion and motivation would be used to remove the child to a healthy environment. Further, care will be taken to provide institutional facilities to the maximum extent so that the child is not isolated and she can be brought into the mainstream.

2. Though ICDS projects have been sanctioned in red light areas the response in terms of functioning of the Anganwadis has not been encouraging. Special relaxations in terms of the limit on the number of children per project, compulsory linkage with Adolescent Girls Scheme and Anganwadi cum Creches Scheme would be provided in project sanctioned in red light districts and high supply/risk villages.

3. Free and compulsory education would be provided to child victims and children of women victims in Government/Municipal schools. There would be free supply of text books, uniforms, scholarships to children of women victims and to child victims under existing schemes or projects. It would be ensured that the schools are linguistically and structurally accessible and accept-

able to the children and women.

4. The name or consent of the father/male guardian would not be insisted upon for the purpose of admission into any schools or hostels. The mother/one parent's name would be enough for admission of a child into any school or hostel.

5. Assistance and guidance would be provided to mothers to institutionalize their children expecially teenage children and girls above 6 years, in boarding homes/hostel.

6. The managements of private schools and boarding homes would be directed requested to keep a few seats in their institutions for children of women victims and child victims.

7. Projects for continuing education, non-formal education and vocational training would be sanctioned under existing schemes of the DWCD, CSWB, D/o Education, M/o Labour, D/o Urban Poverty Alleviation and Employment etc.

8. Educational support programme in terms of tuition, supplementary nutrition and health checkups to school going children of women victims in red light areas and high supply/risk areas would be provided under existing schemes or as part of integrated projects for providing services in such areas.

Housing Shelter and Civic Amenities

Women victims should be assisted for inclusion of their names in electoral rolls and to obtain electoral photo identity cards to help them exercise their franchise.

Women victims as women heading households, should be given ration cards under the Targetted Public Distribution System as a separate eligible category.

Since shelter is the main requirement for women victims who wish to be reintegrated in society, they should get preferential allotment of sites and houses reserved for Economically Weaker Sections in urban and rural areas, under schemes of the Central Government like Indira Awas Yojana and schemes of the State Government like Indira Awas Yojana and schemes of the State

Government as well as housing projects of local bodies and development authorities.

Girls and women subjected to violence will be provided well funded shelters and relief support as well as medical, psychological and other counselling services and free or low cost legal aid where it is needed, as well as appropriate assistance to enable them to find means of subsistence.

Special Short Stay Homes which are set up near red light areas should allow women victims who are pregnant to stay there during pregnancy and after delivery. Existing Short Stay Homes will set apart some seats for women victims of sexual exploitation.

Juvenile Homes would be set up or strengthened wherever the existing facilities are not sufficient to accommodate child victims or children of women victims who are rescued through the three C's of counselling cajoling and/or coercion.

Efforts will be made by NGO's and the officers of the homes to find alternate long-term shelter for the children in SOS Children's Homes and foster homes.

Economic Empowerment

Women victims should be guided and assisted to form self help groups to take up, among other activities, savings and credit activity. Once they have gained sufficient experiences and accumulated savings, they would be assisted by RMK, banks, cooperative banks etc., for micro credit for income generating activities.

Women Development Corporations, NGO's and other agencies would be encouraged to take up training cum employment/production projects in both traditional and non-traditional trades in red light areas and high supply areas to train women and child victims and children of victims. Assistance would be provided for purchase of assets, infrastructure, raw material supply, technical inputs and marketing tie ups. Such projects would be assisted under existing schemes of the Central and State Governments.

In all projects assisted by Governmental agencies, by NGO's and the private sector, women victims who are rescued should be given employment to the extent of atleast 50 per cent of the total number of full and part time staff.

The public and private sector would be encouraged to take part in rehabilitation of rescued women and child victims through providing income generating training and employment/self-employment opportunities for them including piece-work, sub-contracting assembly units.

Legal Reforms and Law Enforcement

The present legal framework to combat commercial sexual exploitation result in revictimisation of the victims of exploitation while the exploiters mostly go scot-free. Statistics reveal that the number of females arrested is roughly four times the number of males in the implementation of the ITPA, The present laws would therefore be reviewed to ensure that the victims of commercial sexual exploitation are not revictimised and that all the exploiters, not excluding clients, traffickers, parents/guardians and others who collude with them, are made liable for punishment.

Criminal procedures would also be modified and improved to ensure gender/child sensitive application of judicial processes and efficient and quick prosecution of traffickers, including summary disposal of cases of commercial sexual exploitation of women and children and trafficking.

Scope would be provided in the laws for NGO's participation on behalf of women and child victims of commercial sexual exploitation to file complaints, provide legal counselling and aid etc. Provisions for confiscation of assets of exploiters, compensation by exploiters to the victims would also be considered.

Many victims are held in debt bondage by their exploiters. Laws including the Bonded Labour Abolition Act would be enforced of amended where necessary to ensure release of victims from debt bondage.

Central and State Government would take effective, speedy

and practical steps to ensure that the existing legal provisions against commercial sexual exploitation of women and children are strictly enforced.

Cases of commercial sexual exploitation of children/minors below the age of 18, with or without their consent should be detected and prosecuted under Section 375 of IPC as rape and under Section 6 of ITPA where the presumption of guilt is on the accused.

Prosecution and convictions in some of these cases should also be given wide publicity so as to act as a deterrent to all exploiters.

Many State Governments have notified officers in the concerned police Stations as Special Police Officers under section 13(1) of ITPA. This has not been found to be effective in curbing exploitation due to many constraints on the Police Station Officers, including their multifarious duties and heavy workload. To send a strong signal about the commitment of Governments to deal with the problem exclusive Anti-trafficking and Revention Cells should be set up and its officer's be notified as Special Police Officers under the Act in major cities and in district which are identified as high supply areas. These cells would consist of specially trained and sensitised Police Officers at every level who would ensure that the laws are enforced to apprehend the exploiters and provide humane treatment to the victims. As far as possible, women police officials would be posted to these cells.

Advisory Board of social workers and NGO's which are notified under Section 13(3) of the ITPA would be reconstituted with experienced, active, committed and sincere members, wherever existing. For other areas they would be notified without delay.

It has been felt that the major raid on red light areas in Bombay in 1996 as had a positive deterrent impact on exploiters who are now way of keeping child victims. However, the large number of rescued children also exposed the problem of the shortage of facilities of their shelter and rehabilitation. Hence, regular small raids would be conducted to prevent commercial sexual exploitation and to unstil fear in the minds of exploiters.

Raids would be conducted in such a manner that clients, pimps, brothel keepers and other exploiters are apprehended. Revictimisation of women and child victims by being targeted in raids would be avoided.

Members of Advisory Boards, NGO's representatives and Government officials who work in red light areas and in other places for the welfare of women an child victims would be given effective and appropriate protection to carry on their work unhindered.

Members of the Advisory Board of Social Workers and representatives of NGO's who are known to be working for the welfare and development of women and child victims would be given identify cards by the Police Department to facilitate their work..

Counselling and free legal assistance would be provided to women victims who are in custodial places.

Task forces will be set up in major cities to effectively co-ordinate activities for the prevention, suppression, rescue, rehabilittion and reintegration in cases of commercial sexual exploitation and to co-ordinate among the various agencies involved. The Task Forces would consist of law enforcement officers. Prosecutors, legal aid officials, social welfare officers, probation officers, officers incharge of Juvenile Homes, Protective Homes, Correctional institutions, destitute homes. Women and Child Development Officers. Medical personnel, STD/AID experts, Municipal Officers, educational experts, Psychologists, social workers and representatives of NGO's working in this area. These task forces may be headed by the Secretary, Women and Child Development/ Social Welfare of the State Government.

Protection and assistance would be provided to victims and other witnesses of crimes of commercial sexual exploitation against women and children to prevent them form being coerced by the offenders.

Commercial sexual exploitation of women and children is operating under new guises like higher class brothels, massage parlours, call girl rackets, cabaret shows, live band shows etc. These would be regulated by raids, bans wherever necessary, restrictions on their operations and revoking licenses which enable them to carry on such outfits.

Serious steps would be taken to enforce existing provisions of law against the production publication, sale and exhibition of any kind of pornography. Laws will also be reviewed to eliminate child pornography in all media, including prohibiting its possession.

Rescue and Rehabilitation

All efforts would be made to persuade and motivate women and child victims of commercial sexual exploitation to recover and reintegrate them in society to lead a dignified life. Effort would be made through awareness programmes, counselling, cajoling and if necessary by coercion to remove all children above 6 years of age, especially teenage boys and girl children of women victims to institutional care in boarding homes/hostels/foster homes/ residential schools etc.

Assistance would be provided by the Central and State Governments to NGO's for setting up of Child Development and Care Centres to provide education, health, counselling, vocational training, empowerment, guidance for recovery & rehabilitation and for institutionalisation.

Remand, juvenile, protective, correctional and destitute homes would be manned by well qualified and specially trained and committed social workers. The child victims rescued from red light areas would be shifted to such homes. Their protection should be ensured in these homes by the officers, by NGO's incharge, by welfare officers and probation officers. The rescued child victims would be kept in the homes and initially be given psychological treatment for reliveving them from the trauma under which they were subjected to, while in the brothels and red light areas. The Task Forces would coordinate among the various agencies involved and public spirited citizens to see that the child victims are properly, medically and psychologically treated, education imparted and successfully reintegrated with their families or elsewhere. This would require upgrading the services in homes, including, providing special training to the personnel in the homes, provision of medical and psychiatric care etc.

In cases where women or child victims are from other States, the department of Women and Child Development of the concerned States along with NGO's would jointly and collaboratively take action to ensure proper shelter, travel arrangements, medical and psychological treatment and reintegration with humane treatment.

Government and local bodies would appropriately facilitate NGO's to locate night shelters and Child Development and Care Centres in or near red light areas.

In cases where women and child victims are from foreign countries, a system of co-ordination through the Government of India and through inter-country NGO networks would be set up so as ensure safe passage, rehabilitation and reintegration in their community in their home countries.

Women's organisations should be involved in monitoring of remand, protective and other homes.

Local communities, NGOs and other interested individuals would be mobilised and encouraged to be involved in identification, rescue an rehabilitation of women and child victims.

Institutional Machinery

1. Considering the increasing reports about and the expanding ramifications of commercial sexual exploitation of women and children on the international and national level as well the phenomenon of sex tourism, pornography etc., which are a growing phenomena, serious and sustained action is necessary to prevent and suppress immoral trafficking and commercial sexual exploitation of women and children. A Desk on child Resource Development, Deptt. Of Women and Child Development. Similar mecha-

nisms need to be set up in the State Governments in Departments dealing with Women and Child Deptt/Social Welfare in States which are major receiving or sending areas of women and child victims. These mechanisms would service the State Level committees and follow up on the action taken on the points in this Plan of Action.

2. The Central Advisory and the State Advisory Committees would be redesignated as Central Prevention and Rehabilitation committees and given statutory status by necessary amendments to the ITPA. The composition, power and functions of the Central and State Prevention and Rehabilitation Committees would be modified to ensure that it could effectively determine the plans and programmes and coordinate among various agencies for effectively preventing trafficking and the rescue and rehabilitation of women and child victims and their dependents.

Methodology for Translating these Action Points into Action

The concerned Ministries/Departments of the Central Government and State Governments would on the basis of each action point, plan the interventions required to translate them into action and opertionalise the interventions.

A consultative process should be followed in preparing plans and pogrammes for the rescue, rehabilitation and reintegration of women and child victims, with organisations working for their benefit.

In implementing the plans, programmes and projects for the welfare and development of women and child victims, the participation of elected local bodies, NGO's Community Based Oranisations, should be ensured.

The Committee is of the opinion that certain interventions by the DWCD in the following categories are needed to fill the gaps in the existing services available in the women and child victims.

•

CHAPTER 7

Violence Against Women— Role of Human Rights

The sound of women's voices is a vital contribution to the human rights debate. Human rights are a human creation. They grow out of the feeling of injustice which human beings experience in their bodies and minds when their humanity is abused or denied. Human rights introduce the idea of justice in the natural order of the world, thereby giving human existence a higher sense and purpose.

Human beings are both equal and different. The first and foremost human right is the right to existence. Humankind is made up of two sexes and this difference is the mainspring of life. The acknowledgement of the existence of two sexes, equal and different, challenges the unipolar paradigm which encapsulates human diversity in the masculine mould and condemns women to social and political invisibility. This all encompassing paradigm, based on military and economic power, science and technology, seeks to impose for the first time in history, a single and unilateral definition of what the world and humankind should be, regardless of the infinite diversity which is unique to our species. At the eve of the 21st century, the eruption of the voice of women is a vital contribution to the praxis and discourse of human rights. It questions and reshapes the prevailing worldview based on the negation of the other, of all others. Women's aspiration I not for inclusion in a sexually undifferentiated society. Women's task and responsibility is to given full expression to their own history, culture and life experience, thus enabling humankind to regain its constituent and irrenounceable richness.

In today's old, the right of untold million of women to a life with dignity is being denied by specific forms of violence and deprivation, ranging from the non-satisfaction of the most basic survival needs to rape and other forms of sexual abuse, such as wife battering, genital mutilation, kidnapping of girls, forced prostitution, selling of women by poor families, repudiation and, most recently, the trafficking of women for sexual pleasure.

The core of the ancestral role played by women in the family and community livelihood is being irrevocably disrupted by the structures of production and consumption intrinsic to the global economic order, thus leading to the ever growing feminization of poverty. Likewise, the inalienable right of women to possess and command their own bodies is being negated by the wide array of legal and practical impediments. Violence Against women is widespread and long standing. It cuts across ages and cultures, and persists unabated despite the adoption of legislation condemning most of these crimes.

In the field of women's rights, the discrepancy between the legal framework and the daily reality is appalling. Women's debasement is still basically perceived as a domestic issue, a private matter. This pattern of invisibility and privatization just be overcome. The violation of women's freedom, dignity and integrity must be recognized as a major political crime. Human consciousness has yet to reach this basic realization. Today no country recognizes the right to asylm or grants refuges status on the basis of sexual discrimination or violence against women.

The present order of the world is inequaitable and unsustainable. Globalisation and uniformization coexist with and engender framentation and exclusion. Humankind is confronted with an unprecedented crisis of civilization. This awareness, deeply felt by a growing number of citizens of the planet, does not seem to affect either the power relations between States or the profit-oriented logic of the global economy. The weaker, the poorer, the more vulnerable, those who do not produce or consumer anything of marketable value, all these become expendable. The present order of the world excludes, rather than includes, the majority of the planet's population. Women are also deeply concerned with the power of science and technology divorced from ethics and life-sustain values. Genetic engineering, with the risk of an unchecked manipulation of life, appears as unacceptable as the expendability of the poor and of the weak.

Women, who have suffered from invisibility and oppression, are in a privileged position to denounce this dehumanization. Women, for so long kept faceless and voiceless, stand today very close to the many who are not seen, who are not able to protect and defend themselves, who are not aware of their rights and of their own value. Women, the peacemakers and guardians of the sources of life, without whose caring and nurture humankind would not be fully human, have the inescapable right and duty to challenge the prevalence of the logic of military, political and economic power over ethics and human values.

The new awareness of women's rights will affect all fundamental political, economic, social, cultural and civil rights. These basic changes in human rights will, in turn, have for reaching effects on democracy and development. Democracy will not be able to conceal the existence of women and men behind abstract universal principles, nor will development strategies be able to disregard women's needs, values and inputs in their planning, implementation and evaluation.

In today's world, the safeguarding of human rights is the permanent responsibility not only of States and international institutions but, more than ever before, of the citizens of the Each. Only people's awareness and involvement, both at local and global level, can really ensure the strength of this emerging human consensus which underlies the cause of human rights. Following the compass of ethical values and daily practices which enabled them to ensure the permanence of love and the quest for happiness as the matrix of human life, women are called upon today to invent together with men, a new more compassionate common future for humankind.

The Global Campaign for Women's Human Rights

Women want an end to violence against women. Violence against women should be declared a violation of women's human rights. The World Conference on Human Rights should recognize women's right to be free from all gender-based violations and take action to help guarantee that right worldwide.

Rape, assault, female infanticide, sex tourism, dowry burning, genital mutilation, sexual slavery, compulsory heterosexuality, force pregnancy, discrimination (in legal status, education, health care and poverty rights), and more...Gender based violence is a universal phenomenon that takes may forms across culture, race and class.

Gender violence is often tolerated and even justified on historical or religious grounds, just as many nations once justified slavery. The international community should assert the universal value of women's human rights.

Slavery and torture have not yet been eliminated despite international efforts, and gender-based violence will not vanish overnight either, but it deserves the same international condemnation. The international community should denounce all violations of women's human rights.

The UN should recognize and affirm women's rights as human rights whose violation requires immediate censure by all governments; assign reporting officials to survey women's rights violations worldwide and notify the UN of abuses; address women's human rights at every level of UN operations; and urge member nations to act to guarantee women's human rights by passing and enforcing appropriate legislation, by ratifying the UN Convention on the Elimination of All forms of Discrimination Against Women (CEDAW), and by assessing the states of women's human rights in setting foreign aid.

Women's rights are formally included in general human rights but crimes like torture, starvation, terrorism, humiliation, multilation and even murder are rountinely committed against women and girls, and not seen as crimes because the victims are female. The dominant image of a human rights abuse victim is a man behind bars, largely because the dominant image of the political actor is male.

No government now determines its policies towards other countries on the basis of their treatment of women, although foreign aid and trade decisions are said to be based on a country's human rights record.

Sexism is a life and death issue-for the half of the world that is female. Sexism kills: before birth (in the selective abortion of female fetuses), after it (in female infanticide)< in childhood (in neglect of feeding and medical care for girls), in adulthood (in complications from genital mutilation in illegal abortions, in beatings and rapes, and n dowry deaths and 'non or killings'), and in old age (abandonment, neglect and poverty).

The abuse of women is seen as a domestic practice, not something subject to outside intervention. The same question arose with regard to slavery and torture. Without international moral and political pressure, these abuses would be more widespread than they are.

The abuse of women is pervasive, and that's exactly why it must be dealt with at the UN level. After all, human rights has to mean women and men if it means anything.

Coalition for Children of the Earth

What is the difference between a black man and a white man? What is the difference between a person with blue eyes or green eyes? Is it rue that all human beings have hearts? Is it true that all people feel pain or joy? Every person on this entire earth seeks the happiness of life. Is there any reason why people cannot live together in peace?

I know what it is like to feel hopelessness, pain and suffering. I know what it is to see your land, your culture, your beliefs, your hopes and dreams diminished before your eyes I know the feeing of discrimination just because your skin is a different colour or jus because you worship the creator of life in a different way. These are only a few of the emotions million of children feel everyday throughout the world. Every single child in this room and everywhere is beautiful and deserves a chance to love, a chance to laugh, a change to play, and a chance to feel safe and secure. I imagine that the majority of the leaders in this world never had to carry a gun when they were eight years old. They never had to experience starvation. They never had to experience abuse or neglect. They never had to see the death of their parents or brothers and sisters. I assume that these government officials never had to go through life begging in the streets just to live day b day.

If they ha experienced these brutal ways of life, then they would understand and this world would be in peace. Then there would not be killings and brutalities against these children.

The children of the world are young and innocent but they possess something that many adults forget at times, And that is they act through their hearts and emotions which means that they come into this world without prejudice. It is only as they grow older and through the teachings of their parents that they begin to hate.

We children feel that our human rights are violated, and we feel that it is vital that we are a art of the decisions that affect us. We next to be recognized and heard. If the children can continue to be united and are given a voice within the UN, generation after generation then can there be peace on earth.

When the adults begin to act as children and love one another, then and only then will this world be exactly what the creator intended it to be.

Issues for the 1990s

For women to make choice about their lives their legal rights must be recognized and access to education, health care ad employment expanded.

World population as of mid 1992 stood at approximately 5.5 billion persons and it is estimated that it will reach 6 billion by 1998. Over the next decade, the annual increment will average about 97 million, the highest level ever. Almost all of this growth, 95 per cent. Will take place in developing countries of Africa, Asia and Latin America. Approximately 83 per cent of the population growth during the next decade will occur in cities. This growth will result both from natural increase and from increasing flows of population from rural areas. At present there are 11 cities with more than 10 million inabitants; seven of these are in developing countries. By the year 2000, there will be 21 cities with population in excess of 10 million and 17 of these will be in developing. Countries, are working, legally or illegally, in countries other than their countries of origin. Each year over one million people permanently emigrated and close to that number seek asylum. The period from the mid-1970s to 1990 witnessed rapid growth in the number of refugees –form 2 g million in 1976 to 17.3 million in 1990.

A recent UN survey of the world social situation shows that while the percentage of people living in poverty in developing countries fellow from 52 per cent in 1970 to 44 percent in 1985, the actual number living in absolute poverty increased from 944 million to 1.2 billion over the period. Poverty and population problems are closely linked. The highest rates of mortality, as well as population growth, are in poor countries and among poor people. If poverty reduction programmes are to be effective, they must address the issue of population growth and provide improved access to quality family planning and health services and to education. The UN Conference on Environment and Development (UNCED) highlighted the interrelationship between population and the environment. UNCED underscored that high rates of population growth and imbalances in population distribution often result in environmental degradation that constructs access to the natural resources necessary to maintain a basis standard of living.

Environmental stress and the reduction of available natural resources translates into deprivation, particularly for those groups already living at the margin. The intensified focus on the environment has brought to the fore a number of equity issues, particularly with respect to consumption patterns between North and South, that will have to be addressed in the coming years.

International migration patterns as well as refugee movements are critical issues that the world community will have to address. It is essential that the dignity and human rights of those involved in such movements be guaranteed and observed.

Much remains to be done in order to improve the situation of women. It is now widely acknowledged that sustainable development cannot be achieved without the full participation of both women and men in all aspects of productive and reproductive like. Thus, governments should ensure that gender specific data are collected and analysed so that development strategies and policies can be assessed in terms of their impact on women. Women's right to choice with respect to major decisions in their lives must be respected and facilitated. In order for this to occur, their rights before the low must be recognized and enforced and their access to education, to the resources of the household, to quality health care, to employment and to credit must be greatly expanded. In view of high level of maternal mortality in many countries and patterns of female morbidity, governments should give priority to the adoption of measures to promote the health and nutrition of women and young girls. Reproductive freedom is key to the advancement of women. They must have access to information and to a range of safe and affordable contraceptive methods.

The results of several recent health and fertility surveys indicate a high demand for family planning. At present there is an urgent need for the development of safe and improved contraceptives for fertility regulation and for effective pharmaceutical products for protection against sexually transmitted diseases. Given the range of methods now available, emphasis should be given to the development of male methods. In the process of contraceptive research, development and introduction, it is essential that such processes are conducted with full respect for human rights. Constractive research and trials of new methods should be governed by accepted ethical principles and internationally recognized standards. In particular, new methods should be tested on a range of individuals in developed and developing countries who have full information and have freely agreed to participate in the testing.

The experience of UNFPA during the past 23 years has convincingly demonstrated the importance of addressing the moral and ethical dimensions of population and development issues. IT has illustrated the need to focus on reproductive rights as basic human rights and on the need to implement development policies and programmes that are equitable and appropriate and that acknowledge the centrality of women as participants in the development process.

Women and of Children were recognized as mainstream human rights in Vienna

There regional meetings and four Preparatory Committee formed the backdrop to the World conference on Human rights held in Vienna, Austria, from 14 to 25 June 1993. The first regional meeting was that of African states in Tunis in early November 1992. This was followed by the Latin American regional meeting in San Jose in January 1993. the final regional meeting was help in Bangkok in April 1993 bringing together state representatives of the Asia Pacific region. All three regional meetings allowed access to representatives of human rights non-governmental organisations (NGOS) who were able to lobby states' delegations and to attempt to influence the final declarations coming out of the three regions,

The declaration coming out of Bangkok, however, fell far short of the aspirations articulated by Asian human rights activities. It sought to dilute the concept of universality and individuality of human rights by speaking of the need to accommodate cultural, religious and historic specificities. The Asian states also sought to invoke the right to national sovereignty in an attempt to preempt what they saw as interference from Western governments on issues of human rights, particularly civil and political rights and their efforts to link development aid to human rights performance.

This is a difficult argument to follow. There is a set of standards accepted by the international community as universal, that is, applicable to all human being b the fact of their humanity. The problem is not to let these be affected, in fact diluted, by cultural or whatever specificities but to evolve towards their acceptance by all cultures.

The three regional declarations together with representations from Western countries who did not have a regional meeting of their own formed the basis of a draft document from which the final declaration was to be hammered out.

The draft declaration spanning 32 pages was riddled with about 200 brackets indicating areas where there was as yet no agreement. Paragraphs dealing with the right to self-determination, the monitoring and implementing of human rights, standards, the right to development as an inalienable human rights, external debt, torture, extra judicial execution, 'disappearances' and arbitrary detentions, racisms, racial discrimination and xenophobia, the role of NGOs in the promotion of human rights, etc., were among the many important matters enclosed in brackets. The document was also extremely thin on specific recommendations and the section dealing with 'Action of Human Rights' was almost entirely in dispute, in particular important and essential paragraphs dealing with the strengthening of the UN Centre for Human Rights and the creation of a High Commissioner for Human rights.

The commissioner for Human Rights. The draft document before the World Conference therefore was fraught with dispute on even the most fundamental principles of universal rights as enshrined in the UN charter and its various instruments, giving rise to a genuine fear that Vienna would in fact only serve to put the clock back. And although the stated objectives of the Conference were to evaluate the work of the UN in the promotion and protection of human rights and to recommend steps that would improve the effectiveness of the UN human rights instruments and mechanisms, many people doubted the ability of the conference to get beyond the discussion on basis principles.

The World Conference was preceded by a three-day meeting of representatives form over 1,300 NGOs who discussed special interest issues in a number of workshops and formulated a common platform for lobbying government delegates. Regional NGO groupings also decided to lobby government delegates on positions established in the regional declarations that preceded the World Conference. NGO representatives also incorporated some of the common issues raised in oral statements delivered at the Plenary of the World Conference. As at the Regional Meetings, NGOs accredited by the Secretary General of the World conference were allowed access to the Penary sessions and a limited number of representative NGOs were able to gain access to the Main Committee. However, NGOs were given only limited access to the all-important drafting process. After much discussion and protect, including a walk-out of the Austria Centre by NGO representatives, they were finally allowed in on informal sessions of the drafting committee but were barred from all closed door meetings. While NGOs welcomed the fact that the UN system was finally recognizing the value and worth of their contribution in the promotion and protection of human rights, and allowed them access to all of the regional meetings and the World Conference, it was also clear that they were welcome only so far and no further. All the substantive discussion on principles and the setting of standards. Took place behind closed doors. NGOs had no way of knowing what their governments were proposing, opposing or refusing to take a stand on. All of the lobbying and pressuring was therefore, possible only on the basis of hearsay and NGOs were dependent on a few sympathetic and well-intentioned state delegates for their information.

In the high powered, specialized and pressurized lobbying process that is a hallmark of the UN system's decision making process, this reliance on second-hand information was woefully in adequate and certainly prevented NGOs from becoming satisfactorily involved in the most important component of the conference.

The drafting process itself started amidst some hiccups. Bickering and delay finally resulted in the Conference working into the small hours of each morning, during the second week, in an attempt to finalize the declaration. Special task forces were set up to discuss contentious issues and work out suitable solutions while the drafter got on with their work. However, lack of time did mean that the 'less' contentious issues got by while the more difficult issues, in particular sections dealing with implementation and enforcement, had to be watered down in the rush to reach consensual agreement.

The section on self-determination was among the first sensitive issue to be debated. While the opening paragraph declared that 'All peoples have the right to self-determination. The Conference failed to go beyond the recognition of the right to self determination of people living under colonial or other forms of alien domination or foreign occupation.' It failed to recognize the rights of indigenous peoples to self-determination or to recognize the right to self-determination of ethnic groups living under non-democratic governments engaged in systematic and gross violations of their human rights.

Another issue that was contested with vigor, especially by Asian states was the universality of human rights. PC98, the draft document, stated that 'regional and national specificities must contribute to the strengthen in of he universality of human rights.' This was rejected after much discussion and the states finally affirmed that human rights are universal. However, they did add a rider that '...the significance of national and regional particularities and various historical, cultural and religious backgrounds must be borne in mind' while it was 'the duty of states, regardless of their political, economic and cultural systems, to promote and protect all human rights and fundamental freedoms.'

Another shortcoming was that the Conference was finally

limited to concentrating only on bracketed paragraphs. The chair of the drafting committee steadfastly refused to re-open for discussion any of the paragraphs agreed upon during the final Prep Com in Geneva. This meant tat a weak statement on the freedom of expression, dealing only with the media and arrogating to states the responsibility of guaranteeing the media 'freedom and protection within the framework of national law'. Was adopted. Human rights activists were extremely wary of states being allowed the freedom of using 'national law' to deal with the media, a measure that could spell danger to local journalists and which abdicated the responsibility of the community of states to set international standards to deal with the right to and protection of the freedom of expression. Activities were also most concerned that the crucial issues of communication, so absolutely essential to the protection and promotion of human rights, was totally ignored in the final declaration.

Another paragraph which remained closed for discussion, by virtue of the fact that it had been already agreed upon in Geneva, was that dealing with asylum, racism and xenophobia—this was in spite of the fact that Germany had tightened its asylum laws in the preceding weeks to deny political refugees automatic right to asylum and France had brought to power a right wing coalition government that announced the setting up of a zero immigration target. Many activists were concerned that the further closing Western borders would lead to arise in racially motivated violence and insisted that discussion on racism and xenophobia within the context of strict immigration regulation and asylum laws should have taken place in Vienna.

A further concern was that the focus on the issue of refugees had shifted from one centred strategies to address the root causes and effects of movements of refugees and other displaced persons' and their solutions in the country of origin. A prior decision also meant that states and NGOs were barred from making country specific intentions at the main sessions of the Conference.

In contrast to the grey carpeted, grey walled, windowless committee and conference rooms in which black suited state delegates made longwinded speeches or acrimonious debates, representatives of over 1,300 NGOs made the basement of the Conference Centre a dynamic of activity and a vibrant mosaic of colour to democracy; self-determination to sisterhood; nationalism to networking: communication to children; Bosnia to Burma; Cuba to China; was discussed in over 50 forums each day. Discussion and debate apart, evening were filled with music, dance and drama ranging from he middle East to Malayasia, Latin America to Africa and Asia, NGOs also refused to limit their activities to the basement of the Austria Centre. They bombarded states delegates with slogans, placards and leaflets at the entrance to the Conference Centre. A group of Aztc Indians danced and celebrated rituals to the sun in an attempt to reclaim a sacred headdress stubbornly locked up in an Austrian museum. White headscarfed mothers from the Plaza de Mayoin Argentina joined hands with the "Women in Black' from Palestine to protest against the military atrocities and rape in war torn former Yugoslavia. Kurdish refugees staged a hunger strike and Sikhs and Kashmiris demonstrated together. On of the most successful and moving events at the NGO Forum was a day long tribunal conducted by the Women's Global Network, where a number of women spanning the five continents gave their testimony before a packed audience to a panel of international judges retelling the horrors of political violence, domestic violence, economic violations and cultural and ethnic discrimination-all abuses of women's human rights. A moving plea against all forms of fundamentalism and religious intolerance ended the testimonies, leaving a never to be forgotten impression on the minds of the hundreds of women and men who attended the tribunal throughout the day. This was part of a highly organized and visible women's lobby that continued its tireless pre-conference work to achieve tangible results in Vienna.

Among the Vienna recommendations were a Special Rapporteur on violence against women: integration of women's concerns into all UN operations; strengthening the Convention on Elimination of Al Forms of discrimination Against Women CEADW) and the passage of the pending Declaration of Violence Against Women.

'The task ahead is to ensure that what has been promised is implemented, said Charlotte Bunch, one of the women from the Global Network who worked tirelessly over a period of more than two years to achieve this result a Vienna.

Amnesty International combined its lobbying and negotiating work at the Conference with a high profile public presence in Vienna. An Amnesty tent was situated in a public park adjacent to the Austria Centre and amnesty organized many public discussions and meetings in the tent that were country specific, open to the pubic, and sought to accommodate those people and groups barred from the Un sessions. They also set up an amnesty urgent action iosk in the centre of Vienna calling on the people of Austria to send signed petitions and messages supporting Amenesty's urgent actions to many parts of the world, attempting to stop arbitrary killings, executions and to protect people who had received death threats. Violations of human rights which continue and continued to be made by the very states debating the promotion final protection of human rights at the Austria Centre. A march from the Vienna Centre to the nearby Danube island by human rights activists carrying cutouts of human figures painted black signifying 'shadows' of 'disappeared' persons, a weekend festival for music and cultural' happenings' on the island, the making of a mosaic of 'faces' depicting the thousands of persons. Disappeared' on St. Stepen's Platz and a demonstration in front of the Austria Centre on the final morning saying 'stop trampling on human rights', where placard carrying activists protested in turn before each government delegation alighting from the vehicles to attend the final session.

However the 'principle of consensus' in decision-making resulted in vague formulations that could mean all things to all people. Nevertheless, the conference was positive as far as the human rights of women and children were concerned and definitely moved forward in this regard.

CHAPTER 8

The National Commission for Women

The National Commission for Women was constituted on 31st January, 1992 under the National Commission for Women Act, 1990. NCW Act, 1990 I a statute having the potential to catalyse all the arms of the State under parliamentary democracy, i.e., the legislature, the executive and the judiciary, though much more powers could make the commission an effective instrument to be of substantive assistance to the aggreved women. When we sit in judgement to evaluate the work done during its five years existence, we would perhaps be perplexed by the spontaneous and overwhelming response its work has aroused in the shape of hopes and expectations as also that of dissatisfaction some cases.

The National Commission for Women is a product of the women's movement in the country. Parliamentarians and legislators gave tended push to the passing of the National Commission for Women Act, 1990. The National commission for Women (NCW) was constituted to perform various functions including investigation and examination of all matters relating to safeguards for women under the Constitution and other laws. The commission has also to review, from time to time, the existing provisions of the constitution and laws affecting women and recommend amendments thereto so as to Suggest remedial legislative measures to meet the lacunae or shortcomings in such legislation. Through its various expert committees on laws and legislation, the commission had examined and formulated measured to fill areas where there are no laws, such as domestic crimes and look into the adoption of a bandored and destitute children, the common marriage bill, compulsory registration of marriages, etc. While looking into complaints on violence against women and also vidation of legal provisions and safeguards for women, the National Commission could take suo motu notice of matters relating to deprivation of women's rights, non-implementation of laws, in order to provide protection to women and also to achieve the objective of equality and development. Besides, it could take action where non-compliance of policy decisions, guidelines or instructions were aimed at mitigating hardship and ensuring welfare and providing relief to women.

Activities

The first and foremost case that of Poonam Balua, may be cited, where the victim was wrongly confined to jail after sunset and the police officer was persuading her to enter flesh trade to earn adequate riches. Almost a secret investigation made by NCW of this case resulted in dismissal of the police official concerned. It was a rare case, of a type wherein the police was fighting its own police vigilance department for having produced and corroborated the evidence given by the NCW. It is important to mention about this case as our first fight against victory gets gender justice. In spite of the fact that NCW has been especially set up as a statutory autonomous body, it is not to be equated with the role of crime against women's cell or an NGO or any other institution fighting individually and collectively for safeguarding women's rights. However, the NCW being the apex body on whom a lot of confidence has been response by the society and especially by the women at large, NCW took upon itself the onus of taking up certain exemplary cases which would have wider impact on maximum number of women in the country. Banwari Devi's gang-rape in Bateri village in Rajasthan has been a case in point. IT is because of NCW's investigation and insistence and persuasion, that the Prime Minister came forward to offer an immediate relief to the victim and also through the CBI to thoroughly investigate the case and book the culprit. While one accused was arrested the other two are still absconding.

The NCW's intervention in this case catapulted focus on atrocities against rural women and Saathins who are state functionaries. This acted as a deterrent against violence on women—village functionaries like ICDS, the Saathins, gram, etc. Another case that needs mention is the timely intervention of NCW in a stripping case of Usha Dhiman, of Saharanpur who was a prey to the unruly elements and land mafia. Strangely, in the presence of police personnel, Usha Dhiman was stripped in public and was not lent a helping hand by anyone including the police. It was at the NCW's behest that an enquiry was conducted, transfers of concerned officials have been effected and due punishment was given. Similarly, in village Kutra, a tribal women named Basanti Bara was elected as the President of the Pachayat and she has alleged the state Minister for Tribals and Women Welfare of Orissa, who came to inaugurate the community centre, started molesting her in public. Her complaint reached NCW and the NCW, with its powers of a civil court, could summon the collector, the DSP and various officials, he victim and also the accused minister. These are some instances that could be quoted as NCW's successful fight again gender injustice. Thee are other instances and cases of grievances that we have received and attended to but the Commission cannot boast of solving all the cases. The Jayashankarpur (Orissa) village gang rape case by the police force was totally subdued by the local politicians, administration and the police. NCW's record has so far shown how party politics, caste or religious affiliations hinder the commitment to help the women who have been afflicted by various crimes. Apart from investigating various cases could investigate an summon witnesses and get the guilty punished through existing judicial delivery system, the NCW could organize a variety of conferences, workshops and seminars, where issues pertaining to gender bias are discussed and recommendations are forwarded to the concerned authorities for implementation. Though the Commission is short of adjudicatory powers, it has the power to persuade and advise the planning process of socio-economic development of women. Its contribution to the reform in jails and especially in getting non-criminal lunatic convicts and under trials released is significant. Various jails are inspected and the NCW is organizing sensitisation programmes for I.G. Prisons, and prison and police officials.

The Commission could also undertake promotional and educational research to find out ways of ensuring due representation of women in all spheres and identify factors responsible for impeding their advancement and growth such as, lack of access to housing and basic services, inadequate support services and technologies for reducing drudgery and occupational hazards, and in increasing their productivity. About 36-40 reports have been produced and various recommendations have already been sent to the concerned ministries/departments for implementation..

In its crusade against discrimination, violation of women's rights/human right and the ever continuing gender injustice, the NCW a has successfully gained recognition by th supreme Court and various commissions who advised the Commission to prepare guidelines by which some respite and cheer could be brought to the unfortunate women victims. The Commission also funds, to some extent, litigation involving issues affecting a large body of women and makes periodical reports to the Government, both at the centre and the State. The Central Government has referred a number of laws that needed amendment and there is constant interaction and consultations with the Ministry of Home Affairs, Ministry of Health, Department of Women and Child Development Ministry of Human Resource Development, Ministry of Welfare, etc.

The Commission has also successfully intervened against the Kerala Christian Bill denying Christian Women's right to inheritance to property. Mary Roy's is a case in point. NCW has decided to intervene in the case filed in the Supreme Court by senior citizens of Karnataka against 33 1/3 per cent reservation of women in Panchayati Raj and local governments. They proposed to challenge the 73rd and 74th Amendments to the Constitution on ground that the aforesaid Amendments are contrary to the equality provision in the Constitution . (For extracts of 73rd and 74th Amendments of the Constitution refer appendix II). We requested senior advocates of the Supreme Court in all these cases to represent the NCW including the case of Khartoonisa Begum's on the question of Fatwa. In spite of the fact that the Commission has been empowered to enter into all areas pertaining to women's issues and problems, the NCW feels that the remote village women still remain outside the precincts of justice.

Status of National Commission for Women

Women functioning in several states of India and this will be a part of our networking. Now there are twelve Commission for women in the states of, Assam, Delhi, Karnataka, Kerala, Maharashtra, Orissa, Tamil Nadu, Tripura, West Bengal, Goa, Himachal Pradesh and Madhya Pradesh. These Commissions are very enthusiastic in seeking guidelines from the National commission and also in feeding us with information on the status f women in their respective States. They are free to refer cases which may be beyond their jurisdiction. I wish that each State police system takes notice of this fact and tries to establish contacts with the State Commission so that this becomes a happy, alliance in search of justice for women.

Not a day passes, without the headlines in newspapers screaming, murder, mayhem or rape of women, even in the capital city of the country. This is not to say that there are not murders of men and children. The country is facing, as never before a torrent of crime, due to various socio-economic reasons not to speak of infiltration of illegal, migrants, besides enemy States sponsored terrorism to strike at innocent victims, be they woman and children or other citizens.

However, the worst-affected in this crime scenario are the women, as biologically they are vulnerable to sexual assault, rape mass rape and gang rape, often committed by ruffians and the criminal factions to settle old scores with their rivals and enemies. Much of this kind of heincous crimes and atrocities have their roots in the drug mafia, foreign patronage and enemy country strategies to destabilize the civilian population, women and children and strike terror in their hearts. Planting of crude bombs, him and bombs, exploiting women as suicide bombers have all now become a part of the criminal pattern.

This being briefly the crime pattern where do we go from here. Arresting of further crime and criminals creeping into society in the garb of respectable or even common citizens and devising various ways and strategies for prevention of crime must be made the fundamental base for grapping with this enormous problem, which is indeed a global phenomenon today.

Objectives of National Commission for Women

One of the chief objectives of the National Commission for women is to ensure the safety and security of all women, as a prelude towards their progress and development. We must explore every possibility for prevention of crime and also bring to book the criminals who have perpetrated such crimes as rape, bride-burning and dowry deaths, But this is no easy task.

Statistics tell us that a women is raped every hour, a dowry death occurs every one-and-a half hours and a woman is molested every hour somewhere or the other in the country. Also, every seven minutes an act of criminal offence against women is committed. There is an alarming increase and rise in crime from year to year, in dowry deaths and marital cruelty. This is indeed a grim situation. Any factors linked to the growth of crime are, no doubt, beyond the control of police. As far back as in 1970, a United Nations Congress on prevention of Crime identified some crimogenic factors, these are: urbanisation, industrialisation, population growth, outpacing the availability of housing, water supply, and other civic services, internal migration, not to speak of illegal migration, rapid technological changes in transport and communication techniques, which aid the international criminals to operate globally under cover of secrecy and thus cover their tracks.

A recent study of the working of the police reveals a considerable number among them are virtually untrained and to able or equipped to grapple or cope with critical situations, particularly due to mass recruitment of constables without fulfilling even the minimum requirements, often due to graft practices. In the process, many recruits with even a shady criminal past and record have managed to get inducted into the police force, both at the Centre and of course in the States, making a mockery of all procedures including routine police character certification. An ordinary citizen has to clear himself at so many levels before even a minor appointment either in the government or even in the public or private sectors, but the guardians of lo often skip these essential and vital formalities looming large over the civilians transcending and transgressing all laws.

In this context the Vohra Committee report of the former Home Secretary, acquires special significance. In this report, he was assisted by he heads of the Intelligence Bureau, Central Bureau of Investigation, and other experts but many of the recommendations, now over two years old are yet to even been debated, mainly because the report has underscored the evils and repercussions of the continual and near perpetual criminal nexus of he unscrupulous politicians with the underworld dons and mafia. Also, over the years the criminals themselves get elected to local bodies and finally attain political stature, with immense evil and destructive powers to use every kind of luxury as perceived by then and mainly young women become pawns in their game.

The Vested Interests

The criminal-political nexus has acquired and sustained such incredible power that they are able to subvert the country's law and order scenario, jeopardizing the daily lies of the common citizens, worst-affected being women and children. Solutions to this grim scenario of crime and therefore crime preventionary aplenty. But it is only through pressure groups and public opinion that the government may be expected to act.

The apathy of police stations to accept FIRs brought specially by women, the women undertrials languishing in jails because of police delays in filing reports in the courts, are serious matters to be attended to. There has to be an ongoing sensitization and training programme for the lower levels of police personnel. This is an urgent need since the police personnel have very often been ignoring the special legislation on dowry, sati, etc. A proper understanding by the lower police force that women's rights are human rights is very essential and important.

We are not for once under rating the various disabilities faced by the police as a system. The inadequacy of staff, lack of modern gadgetry, the various laws and procedures inhibiting their functioning are common knowledge. Moreover the police, which cannot be totally independent of the executive must devise ways and means for a minimum of operational independence particulars in the discharge of statutory duties and responsibilities. The National Police Commission has suggested that this can be ensured by regulating the transfers of officials ad giving them a fixed tenure and also fixing specific duties/responsibilities in a time-bound frame. A suggestion was also made to set up statutory commissions State-wise in order to contain sometimes erratic transfer exercises by eh executive, which disrupt the smooth coordinated functioning of the police force. A band of women constables must be recruited in each district, each town and city, preferably with proximity to the rural areas, to enable them to ensue the security and safety of the women and child population and to check crime and book the criminals. We are product of women police officers like Kiran Bedi, and a host of others, who while doing a yeoman service in the preservation and sustenance of a smooth and coordinated law and order system, continue to direct their attention to some of the criminal patterns,' crucial and peculiar to the women population and provide safety guidelines for custodial-rape and torture, miscarriage of justice and in proven cases of guilt, find was and means of reformation as also through deterrent policies for the rest of the people.

The policies also in a dilemma, for, if they act effectively, they are charged with excesses. If they do not, they are accused of inaction. We are here today, to exchange views and ideas and sort out the chaotic situation, arising out of a degenerating society, which has lost its moral fibre to a great extent and which in turn has generated an uncontrollable growth of crime and violence. At the risk of repetition, one must stress that it is the common woman who finds it impossible to stir out after dusk, alone, even during an emergency, not to speak of daylight molestations, eve-teasing, rape, robberies and murders, kidnapping, abduction and sometimes bride-burning.

The youth of the country, both women and men seen to be up in arms against crime, lawlessness and violence and this may provide the much needed base and infrastructure for annihilation of the twin evils of crime and violence.

'I look forward to the day when half of the police force consists of women. Also, a continuous interaction between National commission for Women and the National Police Academy will, I am sure, lend fruitful results in our common quest to eliminate violence against women and help in ushering gender justice.

Origin of NCW

The National Commission for Women was constituted on 31st January, 1992 under the National Commission for Women Act, 1990. NCW Act, 1990 I a statute having the potential to catalyse all the arms of the State under parliamentary democracy, i.e., the legislature, the executive and the judiciary, though much more powers could make the commission an effective instrument to be of substantive assistance to the aggreved women. When we sit in judgement to evaluate the work done during its five years existence, we would perhaps be perplexed by the spontaneous and overwhelming response its work has aroused in the shape of hopes and expectations as also that of dissatisfaction some cases.

Structure, Objectives and Functions of National Commission for Women

The structure objectives and functions of the Commission, it is composed of a permanent national forum of seven full time members consisting of a Chairperson, five members and a member-secretary. The commission's functions cover every aspect of women's concerns and issues. They range from protective laws and constitutional provisions to empowerment. (To refer to constitution provisions affecting women refer to Appendix IV). Specifically, these functions are to: (a) take up the cases of violation of the provisions of the Constitution and of other laws relating to women, (b) look into complaints and take suo moto notice of matters relating to: deprivation of women's rights, non-implementation of laws enacted to provide protection to women and also t achieve the objective of equality and development, non-compliance of policy decisions, guidelines or instructions aimed at mitigating hardships and ensuring welfare and providing relief to women and take up the issues arising out of such matter with appropriate authorities.

In addition, the Commission could (a) commission special investigations of specific problems related to discrimination and atrocities against women (b) undertake promotional research to suggest ways of ensuring due representation of women in all spheres; (c) evaluate the progress of the development of women under the Union and in all states; (d) inspect jails, remand homes, and other institution sand place s of custody where women are lodged voluntarily or involuntarily. While investigating complaints NCW has the powers of a civil court in trying a suit; it can summon and enforce the attendance of any person, and examine that person under oath, as well as require the production of relevant documents, etc. While discussing on the theme, one cannot resist quoting Justice V.R. Krishan Iyer. In one of his works he stated that: Women's welfare is legislated galore but remain paper gigars since men are to implement it. That compounds the crime, since even policemen are if reports are correct, among criminals who endanger women. Even the law are so lacunose that the judiciary, if objectively judged, will be found guilty...Women must be awakened as has happened in the anti-attack campaign of Andhra Pradesh women. Social awareness is the beginning of radical change. A massive campaign involving the vast masses of illiterate women, is necessitous all over India.

Taking full cognizance of Justice Krishna Iyer's observations and also after evaluating the work done during the these year tenure of earlier Commission, I decided on joining as Chairperson in July, 1995 and identified some thrust areas to bring about perceptible results in dealing with women's concerns. These were:

1. Speedy Justice for Women (through Parivarik Mahila Lok Adalats)
2. Legal Awareness programme for Women colleges
3. Custodial Justice
4. Steps Towards Rehabilitation of:
5. Women and Children in Prostitution
6. Widows
7. Blind Women
8. Destitutes and Anti-Arrack Campaign.

Till the end of July 1997, NCW, through the good offices of district legal aid society the judiciary and NGOs have held about 100 Parivarik Mahila Lok Adalats. By no means is this a mean achievement in that it has handled about 5700 cases. In the field of legal awareness campaign, we have sponsored through NGOs, 35 training camps/workshops coupled with Panchayati Raj training for women. Further, 180 women's colleges were covered to give legal training to 200 teachers and 5000 girl students and others. This again is an innovative step, the results of which would be sustainable and wide spread. Another important area is that of legal literacy for visually handicapped women. With the cooperation of the Sunanda Bhandare Foundation, 60 blind women were given training during 1997.

We are finalising a status paper on prohibition and development of women to ensure that anti-arrack movement is taken to its logical conclusion in achieving total prohibition. We can cite innumerable cases and specific areas handled by NCW recently. These cover the critical concerns, such as, (i) Outraging modesty of women, also involving persons in high eminence. (ii) Atrocities on women, e.g., Uttarakhand, (iii) Dowry harassment, dowry death, (iv) Harassment at workplace (v) Gender based denial of opportunities.

NCW's effort in mobilizing support for 81st constitutional Amendment Bill providing for 33 1/3 per cent reservation in Lok Saba and State legislatures are to well known needing no elaboration. Processing of complaints, commissioning witnesses where necessary, constituted an important function. The impetus for entertaining a few representative individual complaints came from tales of woes of umpteen harassed women explained in various complaints both written and oral that the Commission were receiving both in office and during tours of chairperson, Members and the Member Secretary. The harassed women were running from pillar to post to seek justice. During its tenure, it received a total of about 800 complaints relating broadly to dowry, murder and dowry related atrocities, disputes over matrimonial properties, rape and molestation, harassment at work places, desertions and other atrocities. Inmost of the cases, it as been possible for the Commission to take up the issues with the concerned authorities and persuade them to set right the wrong done. Realising the intensity gravity and volume of the work in the complaint cell of NCW, we have added counseling and prelitigation services round the clock to offer prompt and effective assistance to the agreed women.

Status of State Commissions

It is appropriate that we meet on this auspicious occasion of celebrating the completion of one year of functioning of the second term of the National Commission for Women. We are utilizing this opportunity to launch a series of programmes and highlight issues of Women's concerns spread over all the five days of this week. Participation of the State Commissions in these programmes provides an excellent opportunity for interaction, and avenues for networking, not only among the State Commissions and NGOs and others but also lays a strong foundation for future cooperation and collaboration on all issues concerning women.

This opportunity to welcome in our midst and congratulate

the Women's Commissions of Delhi and Kerala which were constituted after the last conference of States and National Commission which was held in March, 1995. As a matter of fact, the Commission in Kerala was set up only a few days back. We had been pursuing with various States the question of setting up of Women's Commission and had expected several more State Commissions to have been formed by this time, but most of the States have not found it feasible so far in spite of assurances. We hope that 1996 will witness the constitution of Women's Commission at least in all major States like Uttar Pradesh, Madhya Pradesh, Bihar, Rajastahan, Karnataka, Haryana, Andhra Pradesh and others.

The tree-year term of the first national commission for Women came to an end on 31st January, 1995 except for one member who had not completed three years. Weeks, and then months, passed by without the vacancies being filled with the result that only one member and the member secretary carried on the Commission work until July, 1995 when the Chairperson and four other members were nominated. The intervening six months were utilised to complete the ongoing projects and other pending work, drawing up future plans, convening a conference of the State Commissions, organising two or three seminars/ workshops, taking stock of the work done in the preceding years and attending to some other issues like drafting our part for the Country Paper for Beijing Conference. Ms Padma Seth joined us as Member in January, 1996. Last March, two members resigned. Thus, the Commission is now short of two members. Anew member secretary, R. Nisha Sahal Achuttan, joined us only a couple of weeks back. On assuming charge, I made it a point that the Commission work at a breakneck speed so as to make up for he loss of six months. The achievements of the Commission during one year period are many and we are satisfied.

The Commission has undertaken a large-scale programme for creating legal awareness among women. For this purpose, we have tied up with the National Law School. Banglore were selected lady teachers of women's colleges form all over the country are trained in legal matters pertaining to women and they in turn hold legal awareness classes for girl students of their colleges. Another reaction plan of the commission has been to give impetus to the anti-arrack movement in the country. Liquor, as well all know, is a major cause of ruin of many poor and middle class homes. Women's groups in several states have started anti-arrack movements, with marked success at a number of places. The commission aims to bring into a network the virus women's groups all over the country engaged in anti-arrack struggle so as to create a strong lobby against the evil s of liquor. A workshop to strengthening the movement has been mooted. The Commission has also been making efforts towards rescue and rehabilitation of children from brothels and of women forced into mental asylums.

The Commission took up cases of injustice done to widows and has initiated, with the help of NGOs, rehabilitation programmes in Mathra and Vrindawan. With regard to political empowerment, adequate representation of women in Parliament and State Legislatures has been pursued by the Commission and the results are now before you. In a vast country like ours, with a variety of customs and social values, different languages and different levels of education and economic development, the problems facing women differ from region to region. Many of them are area specific some others specific to communities and groups. A good number of these problems fall within the domain of respective States and can best be handled by the State Commissions. The National Commission for Women has to look into the issues of wider common interests. It is, therefore, essential that every State should have a Women's commission.

CHAPTER 9

Women Social Welfare and Media

To tackle this, a family planning policy has been adopted by the government since 1951. But, even after the passage of three decades no significant dent into the problem is seen. The population of the country has since been doubled. That the present situation is alarming can be realised from the following data: "there are at present 120 million married couples in the reproductive ages (MCRA); of the only 32 million or about 1 in 4 couples is practising family planning. The numbers of MCRA will increase to over 160 million by the century-end; by then three out of five couples will have to practice family planning if the national goal have to be realised." It is also crystal clear that success of socio-economic development is dependent on the success of controlling population explosion and vice-versa. This makes the issue of family planning all the more important. Television has enormous potential to promote family planning. However, T.V. programmes on their own cannot bring about family planning. T.V. can, at bet, play the role of a supporter. What is needed is an integrated approach aiming at alround development in which other components like poverty alleviation, health education, raising of status of women, etc., should be there simultaneously along with the communication strategy.

The Government of India has plans to achieve the Net

Reproduction Rate of Unit by the end of this century. "This means bringing about the universal adoption of a two child family and the creation of conditions in which a woman will be replaced by a single daughter to continue the reproductive process."

However, one important promise has to be borne in mind that if doordarshan is to promote family planning, T.V. should be accessible to all the target audience. Therefore, adequate resource should be made available for installation and maintenance of community T.V. sets along with proper provision for place, and meaningful viewing has to be ensured. For vigorous promotion of family planning keeping in view "social development and social conscientisation", the Joshicommittee has recommended the following inputs into Doordarshan:

(a) Provision of sufficient resources for programmes on family planning.

(b) Setting up of exclusive production teams for family planning programmes supported by all necessary facilities and training.

(c) Training courses of short duration on "social development/conscientisation" should be offered to all producers and decision-makers.

(d) the exclusive production teams should be provided with "audience and field research" support.

(e) Setting up of a reference library in every centre.

(f) Making a top official or a cell in-charge of the over-all responsibility of the "specialised production teams," along with ensuring inputs to all other relevant programmes and keeping touch with concerned agencies and ministries.

(g) Constitution of a "population and Human Resource Development Advisory committee' in every centre which will have population experts as well as persons connected with other social sectors as members.

During the nearly four decades after independence, India has undergone an Educational Explosion. The explosion can be observed fro the following data:

Unfortunately, in spite of an unprecedented quantitative as well as qualitative expansion of education around two-thirds of the Indian population is being deprived of proper education which is a necessity. The current educational scenario is best analysed by the noted educationist, J.P. Naik:

Expansion of Education System, 1947-82

	1947	*1982*
Primary Schools	1,41,000	4,95,000
Middle Schools	9,000	1,20,000
Secondary Schools	4,000	53,000
Colleges	263	3,457
Junior Colleges	214	1,087
Universities	17	134
All Institutions	1,65,000	7,40,000
Enrolment	1.47 crores	12 crores
Total Govt. expenditure on education	Rs. 55 crores	Rs. 5,186 crores
Per Capita expenditure	Rs. 2.20	Rs. 74.00
Rate of literacy	16.7%	36.2%

Source: An Indian personality for television, Vo. 1, 1985, p. 89.

"The formal education system in India is now a gigantic enterprise. And yet it hardly benefits the common people who are poor or very poor. Most of them, are still illiterate; a large proportion of their children do not go to school and most of those that do, drop out sooner rather than later. Avery small minority does climb up...But the main beneficiaries of the system are really the rich and well-to-do classes who form the top 30 per cent of the income groups and who occupy about 70 per cent of the places at the secondary stage and about 80 per cent of the seats at the University stage. Besides, the system is not adequately related to national needs and aspirations."

In such kind of a situation, nothingless than a radical change in whole education system is called for. Mass media in general and television in particular, has a very challenging role to play in the process of "radical change". Realising tremendous potential of television for mass education, the status report of the Ministry of Education observes that by the support of a satellite, a T.V. net-work covering most people of the country can offer a lot "to the promise of new educational initiatives. This technology can, undoubtedly, revolutionise the teaching-learning system by en-riching formal education and also by supporting non-formal edu-cation as well as the distance learning system." The recently set up Indira Gandhi National Open University in New Delhi, is a step in this direction.

There exists a "vicious circle" between education and pov-erty." An illiterate person has hundreds of enemy: epidemics, hunger, disorder and humiliation." Therefore, it is essential that illiteracy has to be eradicated. Identifying how media can helping eradication of illiteracy, the Joshi Committee points out: "(i) by neutralising the resistance of the traditional intelligentsia to mass literacy and education; (ii) by winning over and mobilising the patriotic and idealistic elements among them as leaders of the literacy and educational campaigns; (iii) by netralising apathy and passivity of the masses to the question of their literacy and edu-cation and making them aware of its importance in fighting the forces which keep them oppressed and poor; and (iv) by consoli-dating the active and sensitive elements among the masses as leading forces for rousing the others from their apathy."

It is also quite evident that television is the major factor in a promotion drive for universal education and adult education. In fact, T.V. is the "synthesis of all the available aids to learngin."[91] But, the fact remains that television is not a replacement to the teacher. What it does, is, it takes the best teacher and multiplies him into thousands. Through television both teacher-education and student-education are possible. Towards attaining the goal of "education for all" the Joshi Committee has recommended the execution of a new National Plan for Mass Education, which should be carried out by a National Committee headed by the Prime Ministry.

The software for Doordarshan should be so designed that the people will realise the dangers posed by fascism, communalism, parochialism etc. Television should promote a people-oriented education keeping in view the basic spirit and concepts of the Constitution of India such as "growth with social justice, unity with diversity, scientific temper with spiritual values, freedom with social accountability, national autonomy with an open society," This has to be done by broadcasting meaningful programmes.

What is scientific temper? Why should it be inculcated in the minds of the people? What can T.V. do about it? These are some questions very relevant from the viewpoint of Indian society and its people vis-à-vis sound software policy for Doordarshan.

The eminent scientist Y. Nayudamma provides the answer to the first question in following words: "Scientific temper implies a scientific mind—a mind tempered by scientific or rational thinking and attitude. It is rather simple. Essentially it is nothing but a state of mind...a questioning, inquiring, inquisitive, analytical, keen, critical, curious, creative, inventive and innovative mind. It is an 'open mind'. With a friendly welcoming attitude towards chance, looking out for a change without waiting for it to come. It is a problem solving mind as contrasted to 'let-well-enough-along' kind. It is the composer's mind instead of the 'fiddler's mind. It is the tomorrow's mind instead of yesterdays mind."

A major portion of Indian population is bondaged by traditions and superstitions. They believe in godmen, astrology and in supernatural beliefs. They also have faith in religious dogmas. "For most people, learning is mainly the absorption of tradition, and education the accumulation of conclusions. Continuity at all costs is the watchword, and innovation and dissent are deeplydistribued."

A detailed sampling of traditions categorised under three

categories—" opinions, beliefs and customs" is given in the appendix. Superstitions and dogman exist as a consequence of lack of scientific temper. Absence of scientific temper contributes towards growth of revivalism, parochialism, obscurantism, casteism, regionalism, communalism etc., and thus become obstacles to modernisation and nation-building. These are the reasons for which media in general and television in particular, should promote scientific temper through their programmes.

Portrayal of Women on T.V.

As it stands today, the women are a "neglected half' in India. Despite the Constitutional guarantee of "equality of status and opportunity" for women and the passage of more than three and half decades of socio-economic development since independence, they are far behind men in most areas. The status of women vis-à-vis mass media in India is analysed very well by the Committee on Status of Women (1975). Its report says: "The content of communication at any given time reflects the pattern of values of the society. The way subjects dealing with women are treated indicate to great extent the prevailing attitude of the society towards its women. In any country women who are half the population are often half the audience. The success of failure of development plans in education, family, community development, health and nutrition depends upon the involvement and participation of women. The investigation shows that compared to men, women are underprivileged in many ways and suffer from serious disabilities. Since formal education is a costly and long-term process it is essential to harness the mass media. However, incidental studies on the impact of the mass media indicate that women's exposure to the media is often marginal and unsatisfactory. It appears that the mass media has not been an effective instrument to inform and prepare women to play their new role in society. The committee's investigations indicate a general lack of awareness of about the rights, problems, opportunities and responsibilities among both men and women. Since government controls a significant section of the mass media it should set the pace."

So what is needed is building of a "new positive man-woman relationship" based on the spirit of equality, dignity and mutual respect. The often neglected "women's dimension" should be taken note of and made an inherent part of all T.V. software. But unfortunately doordarshan's most programmes as aired now, are projecting a stereotype and negative image of women. They also portray women in a sexist imagery. The Committee on Portrayal of Women in the Media has given a brilliant analysis in this regard which is worth quoting:

"— A woman's place is in the home.

— The most important and valuable asset of a women is physical beauty.

— A women's energies and intellect must be directed to finding the right man and in 'keeping' him.

— Women are dependent, coy and submissive; they are masochistic in their response to indignities, to humiliations and even to the physical violence inflicated on them.

— The good woman is the traditional housewife, long suffering, pious and submissive, the modern women who asserts herself and her independence is undesirable and can never bring happiness to anybody nor find happiness herself.

— Women are women's worst enemies.

— The working woman is the undesirable exception who must be brought into the marriage fold and to submit to the prevalent norms of the society."

Therefore urgent attention should be paid to the alarming degradation of the image of womanhood. The commercial film-based programmes and feature films which exploit the female form in order to titillate should be scrapped by doordarshan. Doordarshan should devise programmes which will make T.V. an instrument for improvement of status of women and equality between men and women. Women should be involved in the process of making women's programmes, but the programmes should be reality-based and highlight the problems of the majority of women as well as socially relevant.

It is quite clear from the programmes of doordarshan that by entertainment it means formula feature films and film-based software. Most of these films generally constitute the elements of sentimentality, sex, violence and melodrama. The 'Chitrahar'—song-and-dance sequences show "a man and a woman rolling over each other down with grassy slope, or allegedly 'folk' dancers swinging hip and bosom."

But the problem here is that T.V. is seen by the entire family which makes such kinds of programmes as source o embarrassment. The viewer retains his anonymity in case of films in cinema hall. In the family. Children, adults and old persons see the same programmes in the same room making the viewing highly awkward ad disgusting.

Doordarshan's concept of entertainment seems to be matching the observation made by Jawaharlal Nehru in the Autobiography, "I am told most of the Indian films, both silent and talkies, do not err on the side of artistry...One discovers with a shock of pleasant surprise how fundamentally and yet unconsciously artistic the mass of the village people are. Not so the middle classes; they seem to have lost their roots and have no aesthetic tradition."

It seems Doordarshan has no interest and time for *Jatra, Nautanki, Bauls, Bhajan, Qawali, Amasha, Yakshagana, Harikatha, Tatwalu, Burrakatha, Ottam Thullal, Villupatu*, etc. In order to provide meaningful entertainment Doordarshan should combine entertainment with information and education. The programmes should be oriented towards indigenous ethics and aesthetics.

Entertainment is a double-edged weapon, unless used properly, it can cause immense damage. Doordarshan has to make a judicious mix "of sound and sense of beauty and truth, of form and content."

Doordarshan should make less number of films but quality films. It should promote production of television films keeping in view the life-enrichment of the audience and social relevance. Regarding foreign serials, the Joshi committee observes.

(a) Foreign social comedy serials are irrelevant for Indian purpose and cause cultural invasion, so these should not be shown by Doordarshan.

(b) Only educationally and culturally relevant foreign serials be telecast with para-dubbing.

(c) Community T.V. sets should be provided by state governments and foreign comedy serials serve no useful purpose of the rural viewers.

(d) "Content and relevance" of the software should be given the high priority.

Doordarshan should act as a "patron, projector and promoter" of tribal art and folk art of India. This can be done by preserving and promoting these art forms as precious components of Indian art (authenticity) and by promoting and portraying these in compatible forms with the needs of the present-day society. T.V. should also promote classical music and dance along with theatre arts.

Information has a very vital role in the process of development communication. Jawaharlal Nehru was an ardent supporter of "freedom of information" which is also perceptible in the Indian Constitution. Nehru rightly says: "If information—including conflicting views and sometimes even contradictory views—comes from every quarter, we are more likely to arrive at the truth out of that welter than if only one aspect of it was presented. The whole concept of freedom information rests on this idea."

But, unfortunately, Doordarshan does not subscribe to this view of Nehru, at least anyone who is a regular viewer of T.V. news and current affairs programmes can arrive at such conclusion. Doordarshan news is essentially "V.I.P. oriented news." The malady pinpointed in Indira Gandhi's speech in NAMEDIA Conference in New Delhi is worth quoting: "The stupendous task of development, the changes coming about in our villages and towns, among our women, our workers and others might as well be non-existent. Editors and media managers seem attached to the Northcliffe formula that power, position, money and sex make news—and that virtue, normality, hard work and humility don't the weak may one day inherit the earth, but not the headlines."

The Parthasarathi Committee has made recommendations regarding what should be the "news policy for broadcast media"[109] and the Government of India has accepted it. The news policy provides that distinction should be made between news and views. Factual and objective reporting along with news making views should only be included in news bulletins. Background of events and happenings should be provided to the viewer, for this will place the news in its proper perspective.

Doordarshan should show attractive news and current affairs programmes. This will be possible by,

"(i) Team work between members of a professionally competent news crew.

(ii) Adequate resources, personnel, equipment and transport and operational flexibility in developing them.

(iii) A higher quality of management which understand the above two requirements and adheres to a news and current affairs policy appropriate to a large country, democratic and developing and with a wide diversity of languages and life patterns.".

Doordarshan should also develop a cadre of television journalists. The quality of news presentation has to be improved by providing more visuals and elements of professionalism as inputs.

Advertisement on Television

In western countries, television largely depends on the money that comes from advertisement because it operates in private sector while Indian T.V. operates under full control of the government. Advertisement on television propagates a consumerist culture. The Joshi Committee observes "the advertising on doordarshan is overwhelmingly of consumer goods and services, which should in the Indian context, be classified as luxuries," unlike the case of newspapers where other types of advertisements including employment, matrimonials, housing etc. are there. An important question involved here is, whether a government controlled-medium like T.V. should promote advertisement of luxury items in Indian context or not. The promotion of consumerist culture by media is one of the major factors of spreading corruption. This is what the former Prime Minister Indira Gandhi believed. She said, "the constant emphasis of the media on material goods, the visions of th ecomforts enjoyed in advanced societies, proliferation of regulations, the pressure of inflation, the breakdown of religius and ethcal constraints, a general rise in permissiveness—all these contribute to increase in corruption."

Therefore, it is clear that since Doordarshan is not for "business television" but for "education, information and entertainment" medium for the people of India, it cannot and should not be commercialised. But, because of the financial constraints, as the doordarshan and the government officials argue, they are forced to have advertisements on T.V.. Then, the Doordarshan should be extra-cautions, and its main objective of a people-oriented T.V. is not forgotten. A better way is to have sponsored programmes of quality. There must be a "proper criteria" for deciding upon what kinds of programmes should be allowed sponsorship. The code of advertising formulated in the midseventies is a very general type and impractical. So, a new code enumerating points which will take care of all the problems involved and promote a "good taste" be formulated.

Some of the sponsored serials, for example, *Rajani, ek Kahani, Quiz time, Hum Log*, etc. have opened up new vistas for socially relevant commercial programmes. In fact the success story of 'Rajaji' has made others to bee-line.

Audience Research

Research and evaluation is one of the significant factors which contribute a log towards production of quality software for doordarshan. Audience research unit of doordarshan should be converted into a full-fledged communication research unit which will study the 'felt-needs and interest" of the masses, and thus help in making the programmes community and mass-oriented. The Joshi Committee recommended for training at three levels, namely: "*(a)* training for freshly recruited investigators and research assistants, *(b)* refresher courses for senior research staff, and *(c)* higher level specialised training for selected personnel from time to time."

In order to ensure that the research findings are utilised properly the production of programmes, a Joint Director (Utilisation) should be made responsible for this. The research reports should not be marked as "for official use only." These should be allowed to be consulted by outside researchers. The important reports should be made public by publishing them. Apart from this, the other important point is, all the centres and Kendras should have audience research staff to provide the feed-back from every nook and corner of the country.

Civil society in India occupies a significant space in the dynamic political landscape of the country. The civil society sphere is dynamic too, and its objectives, strategies, and influence are constantly being shaped and reshaped by a complex interplay of state, society, and the evolving processes of democracy in the country. In this fluid context, the role of civil society in political change has increasingly become dominant—leading to two simultaneous but contradictory processes. On the one hand, the uncivil elements occupying the civil society space have successfully communalized Indian politics at the macro and meso levels to further their agenda of establishing India as a Hindu nation. This project of "Hindutva," led by a section of civil society, is steadily reducing the democratic space in the country, communalising state institutions, and threatening the fundamental building blocks of secularism and the universal criterion of citizenship in the Indian republic, supporting the claim in the introduction that "antidemocratic forces in civil society may be working to limit and even reverse certain democratic developments." On the other hand, a large section of civil society, working primarily at the micro level, presents an alternative vision of justice and development that is embedded in the discourse of empowerment, rights, and democracy. This section has deepened and furthered certain dimensions of progressive political change and in the process has enlarged its own operating space at the local level. This civil society is attempting to foster and consolidate political change, not only by making the state more democratic, but also by employing various strategies to democratise the society. Its role in fostering political change can broadly be viewed as threefold. First, civil society plays an important role in contesting the state, the society, and its institutions from the perspective of the poor and marginalised to further a discourse of rights and democracy. Second, it is engaged in building alternative strategies mechanisms, and visions of development, society, and politics in the country for democratic, decentralised, sustainable, people-oriented development. And third, it plays the critical role of trying to bridge the chasm between institutional and substantive democracy, particularly from the perspective of poor, ordinary, and marginalised citizens.

Our aim here is to sum up the impact of civil society on political change by analyzing, with the help of case studies, the two contradictory but significant processes initiated by civil society that are transforming Indian politics—first, by narrowing democratic and secular spaces at the macro and meso levels and, second, by opining new spaces at the micro level for democratic action for and by the poor and disempowered.

Indian today has a population of more than one billion people, speaking eighteen major languages and sixteen hundred minor languages and dialects, practicing more than six major religions, from six main ethnic groups, divided into 6,400 castes and subcastes and fifty-two major tribes (*India Today*, Aug. 19, 2002). India has twenty-eight states and seven union territories. More than five hundred principalities and British India, with different histories, language, culture, and resources, came together to form the Republic of India in 1950. Indeed, the county's plurality and diversity are strongly reflected in the multiplicity of the experiences of different communities, regions, and classes in independent India. It would be futile to search for homogeneous sociopolitical trends in India leading to a uniform trajectory of change and development. But certain broad developments and processes can be identified that have had serious implications for the country's sociopolitical and economics spheres.

Its immense diversity, plurality, size, and experience of sustained multiparty democracy, despite high levels of poverty and low human development, make India unique. A great deal has been achieved in the past fifty-two years in science and technology and certain sectors of the economy (expansion and diversification of production; the adoption of new technologies and modern management; advances in medicine, engineering, and software development), but there is nonetheless widespread inequality in India—across states, between rural and urban areas, within communities and castes, and between women and men. In 1992-93, for example, infant mortality was 59 per 1,000 in urban areas and 94 in rural areas; life expectancy at birth among women in Madhya Pradesh was fifty-seven years, which is eighteen years less than the life expectancy of women in Kerala, and infant mortality was 107 and 91 per 1,000 among the scheduled castes and scheduled tribes respectively, substantially higher than the infant mortality rate for the rest of the population. India's economic growth has been impressive—it is one of the few developing countries to have enjoyed sustained growth in per capita income since 1950—but levels of human development remain very low. Some 55 percent of children under the age of five remain malnourished—nearly twice levels reported in many parts of sub-Saharan Africa. India's maternal mortality rate, 410 per 100,000 live births, is almost 100 times the level found in the West. Close to two million infants die every year. Adult literacy in 1991 was only about 52 percent, and close to two-thirds of India's women could not read or write. Considerations of gender, caste, and class continue to affect access to basic social services. Despite India's many achievements, some 34 percent of the country's total population continues to live below the poverty line (Census of India 1991).

The progress of postcolonial India thus presents a mixed picture. The country has made striking achievements in some sectors but has failed massively in many dimensions of human development. Certainly, the fruits of India's economic development have not reached the poor, the marginalised, and the deprived. This failure highlights the persistence of widespread inequality and reflects the extent of human deprivation. Illiteracy, ill health, malnutrition, insufficient earnings, social exclusion, lack of say indecision making—all must be viewed as a "set of un-freedoms constituting human poverty".

Under British colonial rule, the state was an instrument used by the imperial Raj for aggressively pursuing its economic and political interests by developing elaborate sets of rules and laws to be implemented through bureaucratic mechanisms or the coercive state apparatus if required. The inherent principle of governance was to secure the economic agenda of the British Raj; the people were viewed primarily as a law and order issue (Sharma 1992: 32-35). All this changed, however, when India achieved its independence on August 15, 1947, through a mass-based, nonviolent independence movement led by Mahatma Gandhi and the Indian National Congress. The newly independent Indian Union enated the constitution of India on January 26, 1950. Clearly stating the philosophy of the newly created state, the amended preamble of the constitution says: "We the people of India, having solemnly resolved to constitute India into a sovereign socialist secular democratic republic..." (Basu 1994:20). With this vision India embarked on the path of post-colonial nation building with enthusiasm and optimism, despite the tragic and violent partition of the country.

To achieve these lofty ideals, India adopted the path of economic growth through planned development emphasising technological advancement and heavy industry. One of the assumptions was that the benefits of economic growth would trickle down to the poor and eradicate poverty. Simultaneously, endeavours were undertaken to create modern institutions for democratic governance a parliament, election commission, autonomous judiciary, and the like. But the rewards of economic growth failed to reach the poor and marginalized, and the prerequisite conditions for social and economic democracy failed to materialized. The political democracy guaranteed by the constitution to every Indian citizen was constrained by the lack of social and economic democracy.

By the mid-1970s, the enthusiasm for national building had given way to agitation against the prevailing corruption, food scarcity, unemployment, and a worsening economic situation after the India-Pakistan war. The energies unleashed by the protests and mobilization on these issues were channelled by the veteran socialist leader J.P. Narayan into political mass movements for *sampoorn kranti* (total revolution) and *navnirman* (reconstruction), directly confronting the authoritarian rule of Prime Minister Indira Gandhi. In June 1975, Indira Gandhi's election to the parliament was declared invalid by a state high court—prompting her to declare a state of emergency that meant the end of democratic governance and led to a suspension of fundamental rights and civil liberties for two years. In 1977, democratic rule was restored.

In postcolonial India, responsibility for nation building, social justice, and economic growth was entrusted to the state. It attempted to achieve these objectives through a combination of strategies: a mixed economy, planned development, social legislation, public welfare policies, and federal governance. This policy led to a maximalist role for the state, which entered all spheres of public and civic life. The state has not been able to achieve these objectives in five decades, however, and the Indian experience has been uneven. Economic growth has been slow, and its fruits continue to be distributed unequally among individuals, communities, and regions; social divisions and hierarchies have not been reduced; human development remains low. The factors responsible for the lack of human, economic, social, and political development are manifold and complex and beyond the scope of this study. Some scholars, however, cite the lack of development of a democratic policy, state, and society—notwithstanding regular elections, representative parliamentary democracy, elected governments (except for a brief spell of less than two years), and a vigorous multiparty system—as one of the significant reasons for this developmental failure.

The brief period of emergency and the emerging notion of state erosion changed the discourse of the Indian polity and irreversibly changed the character and trajectory of the Indian state. In 1980, Indira Gandhi returned to power after three years in the opposition, and her new priorities signaled the changing character of the Indian state and its slide from the "commanding heights." By the mid-1980s, the state had become open to working with outside agencies and initiated significant moves for decentralization of governance. The first shift was forcefully articulated by the seventh five-year plan, which accorded formal recognition to the role of NGOs in fulfilling the plan's objectives, and since then the recognition has steadily grown. This shift was further consolidated in March 1994 when, at the behest of the prime minister, the Planning Commission organized a meeting of over a hundred NGOs cabinet ministers, government of India officials, and several state government officials, which drafted an "action plan" to create a collaborative relationship between NGOs and the government. The second significant shift was to initiate the process of democratic decentralisation by providing a constitutional mandate to institutions of local self-governance in both rural and urban areas. Two constitutional amendments gave uniformity and formal structure to the institutions of self-governance necessary for effective functioning. Above all, the seventy-third amendment formally recognised the traditional *panchayats* as institutions of local self-governance in rural India—a fundamental restructuring of the country's governance and administrative system based on the philosophy of decentralisation and power to the people. Many view the new *panchayati* system as having the potential to usher in an era of change in accord with people's needs and priorities and the power to revitalize a deeply troubled democracy (Behar and Kumar 2002).

Another watershed in the history of the Indian State after Indira Gandhi's emergency decree came in 1991 when—owing to depleted foreign reserves, growing foreign debt, a worsening economic situations, and the growing realisation of the state's limited potential for social and economic transformation—India adapted the path of liberalization and structural adjustment, paving the way for a greater role of market forces and globalisation. It was expected that this retreat of the state from the economic sphere (and gradually from other spheres) would unleash the process of growth and development. But the benefits of these changes, if any have not reached the majority of a population that remains poor, vulnerable, and disadvantaged.

The most significant political change, however, has been the rise of communal and majoritarian politics in the 1980s and 1990s led by the Rashtriya Swamsewak Sangh (RSS) and its affiliate organizations—a change that has led to the killing of thousands of people in communal riots over the past decade, culminating in the genocide against the Muslim community in Gujarat in early 2002. The RSS and affiliates succeeded with communal mobilization by initiating the Ayodhya movement to built a Hindu temple in place of the Babri mosque. (The RSS believes the mosque was built by a Moghul ruler who destroyed a temple on the site making the birthplace of the Hindu god-king Rama.) This movement gathered enormous support for the RSS from the majority of Hindus in northern India, resulting in electoral victories in several states for its political wing: the Bharatiya Janata Party (BJP). The RSS and its affiliate organisations used the strategy of communal mobilization along religious lines for majoritarian politics—leading to the rise to power of BJP, which formed the national government in 1998. The polity is now so strongly dominated by RSS and its affiliates that the country's sociopolitical agenda is being set by these organisations, to which secular forces are simply responding. The state and its institutions under the BJP government are becoming increasingly communal as well, posing the biggest threat to the secular and democratic foundations of the Indian republic since independence.

In this overall context of liberalisation, privatisation, globalisation, growing partnerships between state and market and state and civil society, democratic decentralisation, the failure of the state as an agent for development and change, and the phenomenal rise of communalism, it is becoming clear that the revitalisation of civil society discourse and space in India has generated contradictory trends of regression and hope for democracy in the country.

Mapping India's Civil Society

The process of democratisation of society and polity has varied from region to region. The Indian state's federal structure has also encouraged diverse levels of democratisation in different regions of the country. As a corollary, the development of civil society also varies, depending on the federal unit of state, the level of development of traditional political institutions, and the prevailing conditions for democracy and political mobilisation. Thus civil society is vigorous and fairly well developed in some regions, whereas in others, its space is shrinking. Despite these differences across time and space, mapping the civil society terrain offers insights into the civil society space in India.

In the mid-to-late colonial period, India witnessed extensive civil activity of three kinds. The first was the philanthropy of Christian missionaries, who built schools, colleges, dispensaries, and orphanages. The second category was initiated by an Indian bourgeosive that was greatly influenced by Western liberal thought—leading to the building of schools, colleges, and hospitals, as well as issue-based social reform regarding widow remarriage, improvement of women's social status, women's education, the practice of suttee, and so on. These initiatives found very fertile ground in Bengal but soon travelled to the western coast in Mumbai (Bombay) and spread across the country. Mahatma Gandhi gave impetus to the third kind of civil society: activity based on voluntary action and movements such as Harijan Sevak Sangh, Buniyadi Talim, and the All-India Spinners Association. Gandhi believed that voluntary action and constructive work leading to the self-reliance of villages was essential to free India of its problems of poverty, inequality, and exploitation. Often these organisations were led by people who were also involved in the national freedom struggle as members of the Congress Party under Gandhi's leadership. By the time of independence, the entire civil society arena was occupied by the Congress Party and its affiliate organisations inspired by Gandhian ideals (Jayal200:129).

After independence, the civil society landscape was occupied by religious and Gandhian organisations working on a variety of welfare and development issues: health, education, village industries, handicrafts, trainjng of government officials. There religious organisations focused their attention on health and nutrition, famine relief, relief for refugees, and the like. The Gandhian groups, which still occupied most of the civil society space, started getting government support and funding and a few even became organs of the state such as the Khadi and Village Industries Commission. Many of the Gandhian organizations across the country not seeking government support were under the umbrella of Sarva Seva Sangh training volunteers for social action from ashrams based in remote areas of the country. These workers, called *sarvodayi*, constituted an important part of the civil society spectrum. Many other Gandhians did not believe in institutional structure and preferred individual and group social action (Mahaja 2002:107). The most prominent among these Gandhians was Acharya Vinoba Bhave, who led a movement called *Bhoodan*, which urged voluntary donation of land by wealthy landlords for redistribution among the rural landless poor.

The 1970s were a volatile period for India. The country witnessed the end of a romantic armed revolutionary movement in rural West Bengal, unemployment and worsening economic conditions leading to mass political mobilization and nationwide strikes, and suspension of democracy for tow years under a national emergency declared by an authoritarian regime, leading to a compete transformation of the civil society space. The emergency was used by Indira Gandhi, the prime minister, to suspend civil liberties, introduce censorship and curbs on the freedom of the press, and use arbitrary detention laws to muzzle any form of opposition. Although the experience of a national emergency during which democratic rule was suspended came as a rude shock, it rekindled interest in civil society—in fact, the opposition to emergency rule came substantially from civil society. Under different names, strands, and umbrellas, civil society was galvanised to act against the authoritarian regime. In fact, many activists regard the emergency as a watershed that led to the present proactive phase of this civil society in India.[1] This experience transformed and revitalised India's civil society. For the first time in the country's post-independence history, civil society "emerged in response and resistance to the state"(Jayal 2000:1132).

This socio-political scenario provided fertile ground for the emergence of organisations and initiatives that would reshape the concept of civil society and shift the focus from welfare and charity to development, empowerment, and social change. Many of these organisations were a curious mixture of Gandhian and Marxist idealism. Notable among these pioneering initiatives were the Social Work and Research Centre (SWRC)established in Tilonia, Rajasthan, by Bunker Roy after his work in the villages of Bihar. Kishore Bharati (the Association for Indian Youth) in Hosangabad, Madhya Pradesh, was established to undertake education programmes. The founder of Kishore Bharati was Anil Sadgopal, a trained molecular biologist who believed that "education makes all the difference and it is the most important tool for change."[2] Similarly, Dunu Roy, a trained engineer from the elite Indian Institute of Technology, established Vidushak Karkhana (Fun Factory) in Shahdol district of Madhya Pradesh for economic advancement through appropriate technology. A young doctor couple, Rajnikant and Mabel Arole, set out to improve the rural health system at Jamkhed in Ahmednagar district of Maharashtra.

By the early 1980s, the civil society arena had grown big and diverse. Here we can only suggest the broad trends representing different dimensions of the complex and nuanced civil society space in India. Certainly, the emergence of non-governmental organisations (NGOs) has significantly altered the civil society space over the past two decades. This shift is strongly reflected in the changing terminology used to define civil society organisations—from "voluntary sector" in the 1970s to the present "development sector," or NGOs, clearly indicating the changing character of the civil society institutions that now work as professional organisations instead of the Gandhi-inspired voluntary efforts for social and developmental work. Some think that voluntary social action has serious structural and institutional limitations in meeting sustainable development objectives and contend that professionalism is required to achieve the objective of NGOs. The experiences of the milk cooperative movement led by Dr. Kurien in establishing a highly successful Amul dairy cooperative gave a further fillip to this trend. The government too supported the growth of professional NGOs. The Institute of Rural Management in Anand was established in 1980 to build the capacities of young people for professional management of rural development programmes, policies, and institutions. Later, in 1986, the Council for Advancement of People's Action and Rural Technology (CAPART) was set up by the government of India to provide financial and technical support to NGOs as a nexus coordinating the emerging partnership between voluntary organisations and the government for sustainable development of rural areas. Other noteworthy initiatives included Pradesh, set up in 1982 to attract, support, and train young professionals for rural development; Ekalavaya, set up in the early 1980s in Bhopal for improving education; and the Centre for Science and Environment (CSE), established in 1980 in New Delhi as a public interest research and advocacy organisation promoting environmentally sound, equitable, and sustainable development strategies. This trend was responsible for the increasing number of professional NGOs working in diverse geographical regions and such diverse fields as community health, education, tribal development, women's issues, and the environment. The 1990s saw the growth of professional intermediary organizations focusing on issues like capacity building, research, advocacy, and networking. The Society for Participatory Research in Asia (PRIA) in Delhi, with its wide, strong network in more than twelve states, and the National Centre for Advocacy Studies in Pune (Poona) are good examples of this trend.

The NGOs have become key players in the field of development. Indeed the government recognises their contribution and is working with these agencies to achieve its development objectives. Several donor agencies, multilateral organisations, and international organizations, too, have realised the potential of NGOs in facilitating people-centred development and are working in close collaboration with these agencies. Despite the enthusiasm in the development sector for the potential of NGOs as a significant force for achieving people centred development, there are questions concerning their role, ability, and efficacy. These issues emerge from the evident weaknesses of NGOs. Their success has been limited to dimensions of development that area soft and operate only at the micro level. (The NGOs are primarily working to improve the service delivery system and have neglected their role as catalyst for social, economic, and political changes favouring the poor, marginalised, and disadvantaged.) Most important, these agencies have been unable to induce sustainable development.

A parallel trend in the civil society arena was the development of socio-political action groups and social movements. In India, these are referred to as grassroots movements or "nonparty political formations," as classified by the eminent social scientists Rajni Kothari and Harsh Sethi. Such movements do not have party affiliations and work largely through political mobilisation of disadvantaged communities, often occupying the antistate space, criticising the dominant mainstream paradigms and strategies of development from the perspective of ordinary people. Despite their localized support base and local character, these movements have often been able to affect policy at the macro level, in some instances altering the country's development thinking. Some parallels can be drawn with social movements in Taiwan, which play a significant role in building and consolidating democracy in the country. To protect their autonomy, these grassroots movements usually do not accept financial support from the government or other agencies and employ only peaceful means, such as civil disobedience, for mobilizing support and sociopolitical action.

Various examples of grassroots movements can be cited to illustrate their issues, strategies, and nature. The Chipko movement led by Chandi Prasad Bhat in the hills of Uttaranchal galvanized local villagers to protest the feeling of trees until an acceptable solution was worked out with the government. Nalini Nayak and Fr. Thomas Kocherry have mobilized coastal fish workers to protect their traditional rights and livelihood. In Madhya Pradesh, the Narmada Bachao Andolan led by Medha Patkar has resulted in sustained peaceful protest by tribals and peasants living in the Narmada Valley—primarily against displacement of tribal people and flooding of their land by a large dam project. The Self-Employed Women's Association (SEWA), a union of women workers in Gujarat, responds to the specific needs of poor self-employed women by providing access to credit and so forth; unlike the other movements, it is not operating in the antistate space and often "practices a politics of part autonomy form, part engagement with, the state". Like the NGOs, these struggle-oriented grassroots movements also form networks to enhance their efficacy. The National Alliance for People's Movements was formed as an umbrella group of more than a hundred grassroots organizations to intervene in the process of economic and political decision making from the perspective of poor and ordinary people. The National Front for Tribal Self-Rule (NFTSR) represents tribal movements and communities from across the country and successfully spearheaded the movement for extension of self-rule to tribal areas. In addition to these large alliances, activist organisations like the People's Union for Democratic Rights (PUDR) and People's Union for Civil Liberties (PUCL), mostly made up of educated urban progressives, have also played a significant role in supporting grassroots movements through media advocacy and judicial intervention.

We turn now to the politics of identity movements, which often operate in the civil society arena initially but are not shy of using violence as a strategy for mobilisation and protest, later entering the mainstream political arena through electoral politics. These identity-used movements have significantly affected the contours of politics, democracy, and social change in the country. Movements initially occupying the civil space can be broadly divided into four categories in post-independence India. The first category comprises linguistic movements of the1950s and 1960s leading to demands of federal reorganisation of the Indian union. These movements—the Tamil, Telugu, and Punjabi improvements, for example—were highly successful and the Indian union was reorganised on linguistic lines based on the recommendations of the State Reorganisation Commission (1956). In the second category are caste movements, which have often entered the political arena as political parties representing the interests of a particular caste. The third class of identity-based movements has focused on regional autonomy and protonationalism, leading to violent struggles in Kashmir, Punjab, and Assam. The fourth and most successful identity movement with a pan-Indian appeal has been the Hindu nationalist movement, which has reaped rich political dividends and altered the political discourse in the country.

Unlike the social movements, which have remained largely localized, these identity-based forces have been able to establish themselves as regional and national movements, as their electoral successes indicate (Katzenstein et al. 2001:245). The identity movements mobilize and consolidate support around identity issues and enter the electoral arena—influencing the country's political discourse to such an extent that election agendas have become limited to identity issues, leaving little space for politics concerning governance. And unlike the social movements rooted in a "transformative vision of social change" that have largely operated in the anti-state space, these identity movements have shown their willingness to engage and capture state institutions when the opportunity arises. In this context of their electoral success and serious impact on the political discourse in India, civil society becomes the key arena for opposing identity-based movements and, more important, advancing an alternative democratic and secular vision of India—clearly reflecting the brimming conflicts and tensions within the civil society space.

The worldwide discourse on rethinking civil society in the context of enhancing citizen participation in the Western democracies as well as the totalitarian regimes of socialist societies created the environment for much of the interest in civil society in India (Mahajan 1999a: Alagappa, Introduction, above). The failure of the Indian state in achieving socioeconomic and political democracy and development further heightened the country's interest in civil society. A growing nonprofit sector, international development and aid agencies, the media, and certain academics started suggesting civil society as the site for solving the problems of India. Implicit in this suggestion was the idea that civil society could take on several functions where the state had failed to deliver. At this juncture, it is important to take note of a significant debate on civil society vis-à-vis the state. Rajni Kothair (1988:134), citing the declining legitimacy of a postcolonial state that is unable to protect rights in a socio-culturally plural society, posits civil society as an alternative to the state and equates it with non-state, non-governmental organisations (Dhanagare 2001). This comes closer to the view of Robert Cox (1999). In which civil society is a site for struggle and construction of a counternarrative for an alternative version of democracy that will cater to the needs of excluded classes. Gurpreet Mahajan, in contrast, suggests that such a nonstatist conception of civil society, especially in the Indian context, rests on a flawed assumption that all institutions and associations are necessarily agencies of democratization and would safeguard liberty, equal access to citizenship and resources, and political participation (Mahajan 1999a). But there is a third conception of civil society, offered by activists and radicals, that is closer to Kothari's version. This alternative conception locates it in a non-state (or even antistate) domain of challenge to the establishment in the form of new social movement (Dhanagare 2001). Here we should enter a caveat suggested by Neera Chandhoke (1995:9), who says" "Existence of civil society does not mean that it will always challenge the state, or that it will transgress the boundaries of the political as constructed by the state."

This renewed focus on civil society led to serious debates about the role, functions, character, and potential of civil society in India. Its relationship to the state came under substantial scrutiny. In one conception, civil society is "another name for voluntary associations of all types from sports associations and theatre groups to trade unions, churches and caste *Panchayats*, irrespective of the goals that these associations pursue and without consideration to the way they impact upon the freedom and rights of all citizens" (Mahajan 1999a: 1). Despite this broad definition, the concept of *civil society* in India is largely limited to NGOs, donor and aid organisations, development banks, bilateral and international agencies, and academic. The print and electronic media, which have an extensive reach throughout the country via English and vernacular newspapers and journals and television channels, do not commonly use the concept of civil society, unlike in Japan, were *civil society* was a widely used term in the post-Word War II period. Indeed, its usage in the Indian media is restricted to stories regarding the development sector in the country—indicating that the concept has not spread to the public domain.

In fact, the notion of civil society has not even percolated down to the local NGOs and voluntary agencies in the development sector that coined the phrase in the first place. This lack of penetration is evident from the fact that no standard term for civil society has emerged in vernacular languages, just as translations of this English phrase into other European languages, such as German, do not convey the same meaning. In Hindi, the national language of India, literature and organisations use two phrases to denote the concept. The first is *sabhya samaj* (literally, "civilized society") and the second is *nagriksamaj* (literally, "citizen society"). Both notions have sparked debate at the local level and failure to use these phrases can be attributed to the discomfort of organizations with the concept of civil society.

Their discomfort is due also to the flabby definition of civil society devoid of a normative component. India today has a host of associations that are organised around the principles of primordial and ascriptive identities, such as caste, religion, and ethnicity, and that are pursuing an agenda that challenges the post independence secular, modernist, democratic, and progressive consensus on nation building. Situating these groups in the discourse of civil society remains problematic. Given the normatively loaded context of India, *uncivil society* or *counter civil society* (Chandhoke 1995: 243) might describe these organizations more precisely.

Certainly, the immense impact of uncivil society on the social, political, and state sphere cannot be denied—particularly since the rise of Hindu nationalism in the early1990s. In this canvas, which includes the state, political society, and civil society, it is important to underscore the significance of the uncivil society (groups that espouse totalizing goals and resort to the use of violence to achieve those ends) and view it as an important factor to be studied while exploring the relationship between political change and civil society in India.

Civil Society and the State

Civil society in India has different strands, as we have seen, and its relationship to the state depends on the relationship it seeks. Four models of civil society-state relations can be identified in the country. The first is a partnership that encompasses a range of civil society organizations including the professional NGOs and service delivery organizations. The Society for Participatory Research in Asia, for example, has developed partnerships with the union government and several state governments to strengthen the institutions of rural self-governance (PRIA 2001). Similarly, the Centre for Science and Environment was part of the official government of India delegation at the 2002 Global summit on Sustainable Development in Johannesburg to represent the country's environmental concerns. The second model of the civil-state relationship is that of part partnership and part opposition, a category that includes many of the activist NGOs grassroots organisations, and some social movements. In this model the organisation develops a partnership with the state in several spheres of its work by joining government appointed committees, facilitating the implementation of government programmes acceptable to it, and so forth, nevertheless retaining its autonomy to criticise government programmes and policies. *Ekta Parishad* (Unity Forum) a mass-based people's organisation, has formed a joint task force with the Government of Madhya Pradesh to help resolve the demands for land by landless farmers and tribals but through mass mobilisation strong opposes the forest policies being implemented by the state government and its partner, the World Bank. The third model is one of opposition and negotiation with the state, a category that includes many of the radical grassroots and social movements discussed earlier. The *Narmada Bachao Andolan* (NBA; Save Narmada Movement) rejects the state's development paradigm based on construction of large dams; it also criticizes the government's policies but is negotiating with it for compensation and rehabilitation through institutional and informal channels. The flexibility available to the Indian civil society in developing a relationship with the state suggests the strength of democratic institutions and culture in the country. In the fourth model, the new paradigm since the 1990s, civil society is able to steer the state's agenda in line with its own objectives. This model is taking shape under the guidance of RSS and affiliate organisations, which often dictate the agenda and policies of the state through the union government led by BJP. The union government's ordering the rewriting of history textbooks for schools across the country to suit RSS's communal historiography is a strong sign of this trend.

Despite the presence of vigorious institutions and a culture of democracy, the state often tries to curtail the flexibility of civil society through its repressive apparatus and extraconstitutional methods. Its attempts have been largely unsuccessful, however, and the guarantees in the constitution of India regarding civil and political rights, coupled with the democratic energies of the Indian polity, uphold the robustness of civil society's space. Nevertheless, the state has been able to narrow the space for the civil society organisations that seek legitimacy through state recognition. This would be justified by some on the basis of the Hegelian concept in which the state has to order, guide and govern civil society. Most NGOs and voluntary agencies (Part from the social and grassroots movements) seek government recognition by registering with the government in order to gain the benefits and resources provided by the state. Two control mechanisms have been developed by the state. The first is the registration of organizations under the Societies Registration Act 1860, the Indian Trusts Act 1882, the Charitable and Religious Trusts Act 1920, or the nonprofit clause under Section 25 of the Companies Act 1956, which binds organisations under the laws of the act and gives the state the right to scrutinise and agency's work (Accountaid 2001: 1-4). Unless it is registered under one of these acts, an NGO a cannot apply for institutional funding—seriously hampering its capacity to sustain itself. The second control mechanism concerns the other source of NGO funding: international donor agencies. To control the access of NGOs to international funds, the government of India introduced the Foreign Contribution Regulation Act (FCRA) 1976 (Account-aid 2001). Foreign institutional funds in India can be obtained only by organisations that are certified under the FCRA, for which it is essential to be registered with the government. Through the FCRA, therefore, the government is able to control the autonomy of NGOs.

In sum, then, the state—civil society relationship is dynamic, Its status depends on the interplay between the objectives pursued by civil society and the compulsions of the government of the day. In this dynamic relationship, no clear boundaries can be fixed; only a broad, ever-changing picture of civil society in the constitutionally mandated democratic space can be sketched.

Civil Society and Political Change

Civil society in India is contributing significantly to political change—but in two diametrically opposite directions, generating tensions within civil society and creating a highly dynamic polity. To describe the comprehensive impact of civil society on political change would be a daunting task and would in any case overshadow the significant political change taking place at the local level. Thus to gain a comprehensive understanding of the relationship between civil society and political change, we shall deal separately with the two divergent trends of civil society: one path leading to the opening of democratic space for the poor and marginalized and the other leading to the communalization of politics and state at the macro and meso levels.

One trend of political change promoted by the civil society is toward democratisation in which the primary objective of the civil society is to secure the basic entitlements and rights guaranteed in the constitution to individuals and groups from marginalised and disadvantaged sections of society. Today, these entitlements and rights are respected neither by the agencies of the state nor by the dominant elements of society. Although India's constitution and laws have a well-developed notion of citizenship, in practice the rights of citizenship are to realised by the majority but remain confined to social and economic stratification. Andre Beteille (1999) would view this as a defeat of constitutional democracy. Significantly, civil society advances this agenda by undertaking the construction of the rights of poor and marginalised communities—leading to political processes that sharply question the status quo. In essence, civil society strives to ensure effective implementation of the spirit of the constitution, which has become an important reference point for a wide range of civil society actors in the country.

Another significant feature of civil society is its further democratisation of its own space and institutions. Some Indian civil society organisations are pursuing interesting initiatives to democratise their functioning by making organisational management transparent and accountable, ensuring that decision making is more inclusive and participatory, and inculcating democratic practices within the organisation. Although there is not much discussion about the functioning of these organizations in the public domain, the idea is to induce change and instill the ethos of transparency and accountability by building a moral climate for it. The scope and vigor of governance within civil society can be viewed as useful indicators of emancipation of society from state domination, decentralisation, and democratization of governance. Despite these sincere attempt to introduce progressive political change, their impact, according to many critics, is a local and limited, Some of the factors responsible for limiting the impact have already been discussed. But there is another factor with serious implications that must be examined: the difference in membership and representation among the broad categories of political parties, uncivil society, and civil society.

While the number of television sets has increased enormously in the last 10 years, there is still a long way to do for providing the Indian population with access to television. At present only 20 per cent of household in India has access to television.

- Indian television shows a very small percentage of foreign programmes and the consumption of foreign programmes is also very low.
- The use of foreign satellites is mainly restricted to upper middle class, young, educated persons residing in urban or metropolitan areas. However, the situation appears to be changing fast.
- The main use of television as well as cable television is entertainment. However, there is also a significant use of television for news and information.
- The coefficient of utilization is highest in India.

A great deal of anxiety is often expressed about the on slough of foreign satellites and programmes. The anxiety is about the cultural, social, political and economic impact of these. There is also the anxiety that viewers will be lured away from Doordarshan. My view is that there is no reason to take a negative or pessimistic view of the situation. There are certain technological developments which cannot be wished away. There is no reason to believe that Indian will mainly view foreign programmes. On the contrary, many foreign satellite channels, like Zee TV and ATN, have started showing Indian programmes. This will only mean more Indian programmes, even if they are on a foreign satellite channel. Competition will increase, foreign programmes will be watched, but most Indians will continue to watch Indian programmes.

The effectiveness of radio as a means of mass communication in promoting mother-child health care in Ranchi division of Bihar gets established from the responses and reactions of the women selected for the evaluation study. The strategy to organise group listening at *Anganwadis* was definitely more effective than unorganised listening of radio programmes in homes, this clearly suggests the need for continuing and extending the scheme of organised group listening and area specific, planned serialised broadcasts in support of child survival and development revolution in rural and tribal areas of India.

Women need to be rehabilitated and their emotional and psychological problems are to be tackled with understanding. Preventive aspects of prostitution applies particularly to women and girls in moral danger. An important discord. Counselling services could help the mind prevent their taking recourse to this profession. Counsel in centres should also have homes for such women. In the age of globalisation, sex trade has emerged as big industry. Foreign prostitute are liked in India. This rackets have come up for export and import of sex-workers. Recent cases disclosed show that with relaxation of social values, prostitution is not considered as stigma. In big cities, this problem has become acute.

CHAPATER 10

Care and Support for the Victims of Violence in South Asia

The United Nations Convention against Transnational Organised Crime (2000); the Convention on the Elimination of All Forms of Discrimination Against Women (CEADAW) (1979); the International Covenant on Civil and Political Rights (1966) and its First Optional Protocol; The Convention on the Rights of the Child (1989); the ILO Convention on the Worst forms of Child Labour (1999); the convention Related to the Status of Refugees (1951); the Supplementary Convention on the Abolition of Slavery, the Slave Trade, and Institutions and Practices Similar to Slavery (1956); the Supplementary convention on the Abolition of Slavery, the Slave Trade, and Institutions and Practices Similar to Slavery (1956); the Optional Protocol to the Convention on the Rights of the Child on the sale of children, child prostitution and child pornography (2000); the SAARC Convention on Preventing and Combating Trafficking in Women and Children for Prostitution (2002). The State and the members of voluntary sector organisations have taken due note of the rising problem of commercial sexual exploitation and trafficking, in particular, and violence against women and children, in general, in which children and women are the main victims; Realising that the situation of the victims of commercial sexual exploitation, trafficking and other forms of violence in South Asia is appalling and that the rights of the victims receive little recognition; Anguished with the fact that, in spite of several international instruments applicable inmost parts of South Asia, the victims of commercial sexual exploitation and trafficking continue to be treated as criminals and as liabilities and not with sensitivity and that their rights are not recognised;

Distress over the fact that, barring a few exception, the standards of care and support offered to the victims in shelter facilities are in urgent need of upgrading, both in the state as well as in the voluntary sector, to meet standard requirements from a human rights perspective; Realising that rights-based and professionally designed and administered care and support services are neither adequately developed to meet required standards nor mainstreamed; Alarmed that the impact of trafficking and commercial sexual exploitation on victims is extreme and an ultimate form of violence and that the damage caused to the victims is often irreversible and increasingly fatal; Alarmed that the impact of trafficking and commercial sexual exploitation on victims is extreme and an ultimate form of violence and that the damage caused to the victims is often irreversible and increasingly fatal; Convinced that, along with the international instruments, political will on the part of the State and alert and persistent intervention by the members of voluntary organisations shall create the environment and situation in which the victims will enjoy their rights;

Recommends that the issues related to victims of commercial sexual exploitation and other forms of violence are given priority attention; Stresses that in the field of social intervention by the voluntary as well as the state sector, along with the efforts for prevention, the case and support component should be strengthened; Urges that the Minimum Standards of Care and Support for the Victims of Trafficking and Other Forms of violence are widely adopted and mainstreamed;

Suggests that a regional structure be evolved to ensure the main streaming of the Minimum Standards and to monitor their observance; Insists that the issue of ensuring minimum standards of care and support must be taken up as a priority task;Calls for generous support and active cooperation by the international community, international organisations donors, and governments of the South Asian region to ensure those minimum standards:

That the Regional victim Witness Protection Protocol (adopted by the Regional Action forum on Improving the Implementation of Laws) will also be considered along with this Protocol for adoption, application an wide dissemination; Expresses the hope that the provisions falling into the first two categories (Non-Negotiable and Non-Negotiable but with a period of one year to comply) will be strictly implemented by the government. Private institutions and the voluntary sector; States its intention to issue a handbook for practitioners that will elucidate the provisions of the Protocol and provide concrete examples for its application.

(i) Every rescued victim who is taken into custody at the time of the search shall be produced before the legally competent authority.

(ii) The members of the official machinery who carry out the rescue operations shall not dispose of the rescued victims, whether minor or major, at their own discretion.

(iii) All victims, apparently or suspected to be minors, should be kept a special facility for juveniles in need of care and protection and be produced before the competent authority within 24 hours. (See also the RVWPP)

(iv)A member of the competent authority constituted under the juvenile Justice System shall be consulted by the Police Officer while deciding whether the rescued person should be brought before the Juvenile Justice System or before a Magistrate depending upon the apparent age of the person.

(v) Victims should be treated with compassion and respect for their dignity. They are entitled to access to the mechanisms of justice and to prompt redress for the harm that they have suffered, as provided for by national legislation.

(vi) Efforts will be made in assisting the victim to develop and keep contact with her child/children unless directed otherwise by any legally competent authority.

Protected Identity

(i) the members of the official machinery who carry out the rescue operations and the members of civil society and voluntary organisations who facilitate the rescue, shall take complete precaution to ensure that the facial and other identity of the rescued victims is not revealed to anyone except those who are legally competent to know the same. Particular care shall be taken to protect the identify of the rescued victims from publicity through media and victims shall be protected against their being used by the media for its own commercial end.

(ii) Every victim shall be treated as a victim of crime in conformity with the provisions of U.N. General Assembly Resolution 40/34 of 29 November 1985.

Services

(i) It should be ensured that the victim is immediately taken to a certified place of safety after the raid. The victims should never be kept overnight in the police station. (See also the RVWPP)

(ii) It is to be ensured that a social worker or a support person, preferably a female, is present when the girls are being interviewed by the police officers after the rescue.

(iii) The Services for socio-psychological well-being shall start immediately on rescue or at the first helping contact with the victims and shall also include social counselling for therapeutic intervention.

(iv) Immediate medical examination of all the rescued victims and the accused/other persons taken into custody by the police shall be conducted within 48 hours of the rescue of a victim or arrest of the accused.

(v) The rescued victims shall be freely and unconditionally provided with professional medical (physical and mental) assistance and professional counseling immediately after the rescue.

(vi) The rescued victims shall be freely and unconditionally provided professional legal assistance immediately after the rescue.

Transfer

(i) The victim should not be travelling in the same vehicle with the offenders, the accused or their representatives. This is valid at all stages from rescue to prosecution and social reintegration.

Recovery

(i) At the time of search the trafficked person should be helped by the rescue team to recover her personal belongings.

(ii) At the time of search the trafficked person should be helped by the rescue tam to recover children. Wherever possible and appropriate, children will be kept with their mothers.

(iii) At the time of the search, the trafficked person should be helped by the rescue team to recover her documents such as identity papers (ration card, passport, school certificate, photographs) and any other documents that can help her establish her identity and possessions.

Restitution

(i) When compensation is not fully available from the offender or other sources, the State should endeavour to provide financial compensation to:

(a) the victims who have sustained significant bodily injury or impairment of physical or mental health as a result of serious crimes;

(b) the family, the particular the dependents of persons who have died or become physically or mentally incapacitated as a result of such victimisation.

(ii) the State along with its partners shall ensure assistance, guidance and direction to trafficked women, particularly with regard to the vulnerability of their children to trafficking and abuse, to avail facilities such as sponsorship, foster care, night and day care shelters and residential care for their children, especially girl children, and preference to be given to these vulnerable children in hostels/institutions and educational institutions. In certain circumstances, the children of victims need to be protected from their own family/guardians (see also the RVWPP).

(iii) Compensation by exploiters to the victims should be considered. The assets and funds confiscated during anti-trafficking operations and investigations should be used to fund future anti-trafficking programmes and operations. (see also the RVWPP)

Homes/Other Residential Institutions

(i) A Shelter Home (Rescue/Protective etc., for minors and majors) should be available at least at the intra-country level (i.e., for each/or for a group of districts) and/or within a vehicular travel time of a maximum of three hours.

(ii) Where officially designated Rescue/Protective Homes do not exist, other residential institutions which meet the minimum standards specified in this Protocol may be additionally and temporarily authorised to function as rescue/ Protective Homes for this specific purpose.

(iii) The Home's location needs to be consistent with its purpose and function.

(iv) It is essential that children rescued from streets are located in a place which is removed from the red light areas, in order to minimise the risk to their safety and to facilitate rehabilitation. The accommodation should be secure.

(v) The Home should be located in an area which is well connected with

(a) physical communication facilities

(b) telephones including STDs/ISDs

(c) electronic communication

(d) wireless communication

(vi) The location should be well-connected with other amenities such as water, electricity, sanitation, approach road, etc.

(vii) The location should be well connected with other civic amenities such as institutions for primary and secondary education, recreation facilities, hospital, police station, market, post office and banks.

(viii) The location should be, as far as possible, free from known proneness to any natural calamities and disasters such as earthquakes, cyclones, landsides, floods, wild life attacks.

(ix) The location should be as far as possible free form known proneness to any disasters such as crimes, riots, industrial disasters, nuclear, water, air and noise pollution.

(x) The location and the physical environment of the Home shall be clean, pollution free and well ventilated.

(xi) The physical, social and cultural environment of the shelter and other places providing care and support services should be adequately growth stimulating.

Design

(i) The home should be designed/altered in such a way that it gives a friendly appearance.

(ii) The Home should be designed/altered with special consideration to the

(a) common and special needs of the persons it is meant to accommodate

(b) Physical and mental status of the persons it is meant to accommodate (e.g. persons with special physical needs, debilitating conditions and other special needs).

(iii) Where the Home is meant to accommodate children/women with special needs, suitable aids and adaptations, and any special furniture or equipment should be provided to enable the residents to live as normal a life as possible and should be designed/altered by adhering to the recommendations of a qualified occupational therapist.

(iv) The Home should be designed/altered in such a way that the chances of accidents and accidental injuries are identified and minimised.

(v) The home should be designed/altered in such a way as to completely and satisfactorily meet all the requirements/recommendations/ad standards specified by the relevant authority such as:

(a) local municipal authority

(b) building and construction control authority

(c) Fire fighting service

(d) public health authority

(Clearances from all these authorities should be secured.)

(vi) The home should be designed/altered in such a way that if it shares the premises or is in the vicinity of any premises where public visits are common, the Home ensures that the privacy of the resident victims is not compromised, and that there is adequate physical separation between the two areas so that members of the public do not accidentally enter the premises of the Home.

(vii) The building and the premises of the Home shall have sufficient natural light as well as artificial light at night, on special occasions, and at special locations.

(viii) The building and the premises of the Home shall be free of abnormal noise pollution.

(ix) The design, the access, easements, privacy structures, bathing and washing arrangements, recreation arrangements, etc. are designed or altered appropriately by taking into consideration gender-based needs.

Safety

(i) The Home's premises shall not be used for functions unrelated to the Home which compromise or have an adverse effect on the care of children/women.

(ii) Considering the nature of the crime committed with respect to the victims, it is important that the shelter is well protected and given access only to certain authorized individuals and after due scrutiny. Under no circumstance the exploiters, their representatives, any other offenders, or persons detailed under a criminal charge should get access to the victim placed in the shelter.

(iii) Physical restrictions on normal movement within the home (*e.g.*, stair gates or high handles on doors) are used only in relation to a child where the restriction has been agreed within their placement plan (and care plan if appropriate) and are used only where necessary to satisfactorily safeguard and promote that child's welfare. Such restrictions for one child should not impose similar restrictions on other children/women.

(iv) A rescued victim or a person seeking shelter must be placed in a safe and well provided shelter for an adequate period of time to facilitate all the other subsequent services for the victim.

(v) The safety/risk assessment in relation to the Home's premises and grounds should be carried out, recorded in writing and regularly reviewed and shall precede the sanctioning of the license/permission for a premise as shelter home. Permission shall be granted by the competent authority after ensuring that the sources of danger to the victim residents are adequately identified and eliminated whether ever possible. Where complete elimination of these dangers is not possible care shall be taken to work out a plan to minimise the effect of the danger and to handle the situation in case any danger befalls.

(vi) The safety/risk assessment in relation to victims known and likely activities, the potential for bullying and abuse within and outside of the Home and where applicable the impact of emergency admissions on the victims shall also be carried out, recorded in writing and regularly reviewed by the organisation running the Home in consultation with subject matter experts.

(vii) The shelter home authority shall evolve a Crisis Management Plan (CMP) to address a range of foreseeable crises (*e.g.*, death, outbreaks of illness, fires, serious allegations or complaints, significant accidents, staff shortage, and control problems within or outside the home).

(viii) The home shall be insulted against indiscriminate access/ entry of unauthorised individuals.

(ix) Authorised individuals and other visitors shall be given access to the Home only after they undergo a proper scrutiny as well as make and entry into a register that includes the details of their identity, and an authorisation letter or other evidence to prove the identity of the visitor and purpose of the visit.

Space

Each victim shall have a separate single bed or his /her own area in a double or triple room of a suitable size, with a suitable bed or bedding, seating, storage for clothes, lockable or otherwise safe storage for personal possessions, a window with sufficient light for study and other work.

Staff sleeping rooms not be a part of the communal living area (except in case of very young or sick children) but should be located close to the victims bedrooms to respond to night time needs.

The home shall appoint staff only after adequate screening about the past record of the staff, ensuring that the staff has not shown any particular behaviour in the past that could be potent source of danger *e.g.*, psychiatric disorders casing violence or self destructive behaviour, is not is not suffering from substance addiction habit (including tobacco and alcohol) exhibits abusive behavior, etc. Full care shall be taken not to appoint any personal habituated to dangerous drugs.

Environment

The Home shall ensure complete cleanliness of the premises. A worm environment shall be evolved and nurtured in shelter homes and other places of service delivery which will reduce alienation and further a sense of belonging among the victims.

Every victim shall be provided needs-based, sustained, professionally designed and delivered services aimed at the overall psycho-social wellbeing specifically coverign social case work, psychotherapeutic counselling, as well as psychiatric treatment with a scientific assessment preceding it and with an appropriate follow-up.

Baths/toilets shall meet the needs of the residents in numbers and standards. It is suggested that there be one toilet for every 6 to 8 children and minor residents and per 4 to 6 adult victims.

Bathrooms toilets, showers are sited and designed to take account of the victim's needs for privacy, dignity, safety and any special needs, and are readily accessible from the sleeping and recreation area of the home.

Care staff should be able to open the doors to bathrooms, showers and toilets from the outside in case of emergency.

The Home shall ensure that the victims are provided with adequate nutrition. The Home shall ensure that a special diet is provided to pregnant and lactating victims and to those recommended for special diet. The Home shall provide wholesome and clean food to the victims. The menu should preferably be decided and revised jointly by the victims and the management under the guidance of subject matter specialists such as physicians and nutritionists and within the framework laid down by them. The menu shall take into account the cultural, ethnic and religious backgrounds of the victims. The Home shall ensure that the staff and victims who are involved in preparing food, receive appropriate training and are properly supervised in safe food handling and hygiene. The Home shall ensure the regular supply of adequate clean and safe drinking water easily accessible to the victims. The Home shall ensure regular supply of adequate clean and safe water easily accessible to the victims for all other purposes such as washing, bathing, etc. The Home shall ensure that professional medical advice and interventions are sought if a victim persistently refuses to eat and for those who overeat or have other eating disorders. The Home shall ensure that the dining rooms and their furnishings are suitable for the numbers and needs of victims and staff. Food shall be prepared in a kitchen which conforms to adequate standards of hygiene. Separate dining space shall be maintained to provide meals within a specific time-frame. Food shall be stored in safe and hygienic spaces and away from cleaning agents and pesticides.

Clothing (i) Victims shall be provided with clothes free of cost at least twice a year including two sets of school uniforms where applicable. They should be encouraged ad enabled to choose their own clothes and personal requisites within a broader framework and have these needs fully met. (ii) Homes shall not impose a uniform on the resident victims in day to day living. Uniforms may be enforced for special activities such as drill, schooling, sports, etc.

No victim shall be forced to follow a common hair-style. Victims shall have freedom to maintain their own hair style. The authorities shall interfere, suggest to modify, and/or enforce that the victim give up any particular hair style, if it is assessed and recorded to be dangerous or unsuitable on grounds of health, hygiene, certain minimum standards of decency in public life or becoming a source of ill health or annoyance to the others residing in the same premises.

The victim shall be helped to obtain and preserve the necessary documents and other material parameters of establishing her/his identity such as birth certificate, domicile certificate, ration card and school leaving certificate.

The Home shall attempt to establish the human parameters and referents of the identify of the victim such as the whereabouts of family members, community members, relatives, next of kin, in order to help the victim assert her/his rights, entitlements and redress her/his grievances.

Each Home shall make the adult victims aware that they can have access to their files. In case of minor victims the access will be given under supervision of a representative of/with a specific permission from the semi-judicial competent supervising body/ constituted under the juvenile justice system.

Reception/Orientation

Each Home shall maintain a guide-book containing map, design, access to the Home as well as the purposes, procedure and policy of the Home. Each Home shall maintain a guidebook that describes how a child can secure access to an independent advocate and how to make a compliant. The staff of the Home and the visiting experts whose services are hired/used by the Home shall be familiar with the contents of the guidebook. Every resident victim shall be properly and elaborately oriented to the physical and managerial arrangements and procedures of the Home and the services provided therein. Each Home shall have mainstreamed procedures for introducing the residents, the staff and the other resident children living there. The resident victim shall be oriented to the work expected of the staff. The Home shall attempt to allow the children and minor victims to bring in and keep with them their favorite soft toy, favorite books, and play items, except live pets and weaponry toys, etc. – under supervision. The procedures for leaving, covering both the planned and emergency departures, shall be made known to the victim residents.

(a) facilities for periodic health check-ups by a registered medical practitioner, counselor and a clinical psychologist, referral to external medical experts, hospitals, facilities for hospitalisation, and funds. (b) arrangements for preventive, curative, rehabilitative, therapeutic treatment, and (c) arrangements for environmental cleanliness and control of communicable diseases.

The Home shall provide adequate professional medical services, including physical and psychiatric services, in order to nutigate the residents sufferings and to promote integrated comprehensive health care.

Each Home shall have a weekly checkup visit by a visiting general physician.

Each Home shall have sick bay with basic medicines and first aid equipments.

Each Home shall have arrangements to promptly avail the services of an ambulance.

The psychological health of the women and child victims as well as children of the women victims is endangered due to the circumstances of their exploitation. Psychological counselling services shall be provided on a part-time basis in health care centers.

The Homes shall take into account the fact that the victims of trafficking and other forms of violence often suffer from a serious damage to their self-image, self-confidence and self-identity and that the victim may adopt a faulty and self-destructive identity such as that of a criminal offender, or a fallen person. The Home shall work to help the victim to gain/regain a positive self identity.

Each Home shall have a First Aid Kit/arrangements and staff trained to administer First Aid around the clock.

The Home shall maintain and keep updating the contents of the First Aid Kit. The first Aid Kit shall be kept easily accessible to the staff and other professionals of the Home. The Home shall install a system to immediately identify any tampering or damager to the Kit and shall replace/correct the Kit within 24 hours on noticing the damage or tampering.

Each Home shall have arrangements for escorts and by-standers in case of hospitalisation of its resident victims.

The Home shall ensure that the health records shall be a part of the Personnel File maintained for each victim. The report on the HIV status of the victim shall be maintained confidential.

Crisis Handling Training

The State shall evolve a crisis handling plan in consultation with legal and other subject matter experts as well as with the participation of the representatives of the Homes (e.g. earthquake, fire on the campus, electrocution, suicide attempt, or sudden death).

Each Home shall keep a list of possible crises and the staff shall be trained in handling those crises.

Behaviour Management and Discipline

Peer group discussions should be encouraged to raise issues affecting day-to-day living such as bullying, abusive language, fighting, and sexual exploitation.

Victim residents of the Home shall be assisted to evolve a socially acceptable behaviour through encouragement of acceptable behaviour.

Food deprivation, confinement or any form of physical punishment shall not be used as forms of punishment for the victims. The Home shall ensure that the members of its staff respond positively to acceptable behaviour, and that where the behaviour of the victim residents is regarded as unacceptable by staff, it is responded to by constructive, acceptable and known disciplinary measures approved by the competent authority.

The Home shall evolve and mainstream a clear written policy, procedures and guidelines for its staff, comprising of a code of conduct setting out the permissible control, disciplinary and restraint measures and emphasizing the need to reinforce positive messages to the victim for the achievement of acceptable behaviour.

Measures of control and disciplinary measures shall be based on establishing positive relationships with the victims that are designed to help them. Such measures shall be fair and applied consistently. The Home shall encourage reparation and restitution and reduce the likelihood of negative behaviour becoming the focus of attention and subsequent disruption.

Any measures taken to respond to unacceptable behaviour should be appropriate to the age, understanding and individual needs of the victim, for example taking into account that unacceptable or challenging behaviour may be the result of unpleasant experiences, unfair treatment , illness, bullying, certain disabilities such as autism, or communication difficulties.

Sanctions and physical restraint when inevitable shall not be excessive or unreasonable.

Physical restraint shall only be used to prevent likely injury to the victim concerned or to others, or likely serious damage to property. It shall not be used as a punishment, as a means to enforce compliance with instructions, or in response to challenging behaviour which does not give rise to a reasonable expectation of injury to someone or of serious damage to property.

In case of the use of physical restraint on a minor by an adult, a record shall be kept in a separate bound and numbered book, which shall mention the name of the minor, the date, time and location, details of the behaviour requiring use of restraint, the nature of the restraint used, the duration of the restraint, the name of the staff member(s) using restraint, the name(s) of any other staff, children/ women or other persons present, the effectiveness and any consequences of the restraint, any injuries caused to or reported by the victim or any other person, and the signature of a person authorized by the registered person to make the record.

Similar records shall be kept in cases of sanctions. The Home shall regularly revive the record books to monitor compliance with the Home's policy, procedure and guidance and to identify any patterns in incidents warranting disciplinary or restraint action.

(xiii) The Home shall record any comment on the appropriateness of the individual use of sanctions or use of restraint, together with any subsequent action taken, and endorse against each entry to confirm that monitoring has taken place.

(xiv) The staff and the victims and their minor dependents (living in the Home) shall be made aware that each individual has rights and responsibilities in relation to those who live in the home, those who work there, as well as the open community.

(xv) Where there has been physical intervention, the victim shall have the right to be examined by a registered nurse or medical practitioner within 24 hours.

(xvi) All victims, including children and mlnor resident victims, hall be given an opportunity to discuss incidents and express their views either individually or in a regular forum or house meeting where unsafe behaviour can be discussed.

(xvii) In situations where disciplinary measures or restraint are used, the victims shall be encouraged to have their views recorded.

Faith

Under no circumstances shall the dependence of the victim be used to transfer any particular faith system to the victim. The Home shall help the victim to identify the faith system she/he belongs to in case she/he expresses the need to know the same.

The Home shall not make its services conditional upon the victim belonging to any particular faith system. The services of the Home shall not be traded against or be provided in exchange of the faith system of the victim. Children and minor victims shall be encouraged to select the faith system they wish to belong to, or change their faith system only after they become adults and cease to depend upon the Home for their care, protection or maintenance.

Home shall recognise the fact that the victims placed with them are of the victims of multiple sexual offences and extreme insecurity and could have become, or been made by their exploiters, dependent on drugs ranging from nicotine to hard narcotics.

The Home shall be equipped to handle the cases of such drug dependence or addiction among the victims.

The Home shall make every attempt to offer required professional assistance to the victim to overcome the problem of drug dependence/addiction. Adequate recreation shall be regarded as a basic need and a right of the victim as well as an essential component in the healthy personality development of any person including the victim and not as a luxury service to be provided if and when affordable in terms of item and resources.

Leisure interests and areas in which a victim has special talents or abilities are considered within the victim's placement plan, and where applicable, at care planning meetings and reviews. Consideration should be given as to how they will be encouraged and financially supported.

The Home shall ensure that there is a proper balance between free and controlled time in the structure of the day (taking into account the school day or those homes that comprise schools). Free time activities shall reflect the choices of the victims, and the victims shall be allowed to do nothing in particular at times.

Leisure activities whether closely supervised or not shall take into account the safety of children at all times and where substantial or unusual hazards are involved, a recorded risk assessment shall be made in advance.

The Home shall ensure that the victims actively, regularly, and substantially participate in decision-making as regards cultural events, trips, and outings, taking into consideration the best interest of the victims, the professional opinion, the higher principles of care and support as well as the law of the land.

The Home shall ensure that the victims have access to, and a choice in, the selection of newspapers, books and magazines subject to their suitability, and that children have access to suitable toys, music, books and games.

Consideration shall be given to the individual circumstances of children in watching videos and television, and in using computer games and accessing in the internet. Videos, games and computer games may be watched/played only by children of the intended age range. No Home meant for residents below 18 years of age shall have any videos or games certified as suitable only for persons above 18 year. Systems and policies should be in place to safeguard children when computer networking or on the internet and also to prevent the home from becoming dominated by the use of television and computers.

Access to Victims

Access to victims must be under the supervision of the Child Welfare Committee or the Organisation or any other competent authority dealing with the issues of women and/or children, of the area as the case may be. A social worker must accompany the victim whenever she leaves the place of safety. (see also the RVWPP).

Education shall be regarded as right of every individual in the Home. Every victim and their minor dependants shall be helped in every possible way to obtain formal education free of cost, which includes free supply of text books, uniforms, transport and scholarships to victims and their school going children. Victims and their minor dependents shall be provided with essential educational material and supportive educational services such as coaching, tuitions, supplementary education, and special education in order to help them complete minimal formal education that, besides helping them develop their personality, can also qualify them to undertake appropriate vocational training, preferably as much as they can and wish to take for self-fulfillment. Where such education is not possible for certain unavoidable circumstances as well as in addition to the formal education– Life Skills Education shall be provided. Literacy classes may be introduced where formal education is not possible. The Home shall maintain a file on the victims and their minor dependants containing their Personal Educational Plan (PEP) setting out a record of their educational achievements, needs and aspirations. (See also provisions under the Chapter: Case Management) It should be ensured that the schools are linguistically and structurally accessible and acceptable in terms of distance, physical accessibility, transport, etc. to the children and women. A Play and Learn Approach for the traumatized children shall be introduced that covers Play Therapy based on the educational services so as to ensure the right to education of those victims. An adequate number of trained teachers shall be made available to ensure qualitative educational services for the victims.

Every attempt shall be made to ensure early entry/re-entry of the suitable resident into the informal educational system. In the absence of a child resident's parents, the staff of the Home shall attend the parents' (guardians) meetings and such other school events which are normally expected to be attended by the parents of other children at the school. The staff will make a record in the file of the meetings and their outcome.

Life Skill Education

Besides general education, the Home shall provide to the victims and their minor dependants living in the Home Life Skills Education as an integral part of the self learning approach.

(i) No victim shall be submitted to and every victim shall be protected against any unethical, illegal and uninformed medical testing for HIV/AIDS/STD as it violates their rights.

(ii) The victim shall not be compelled to reveal the name of the father of her child for the purpose of the child's admission into any schools or hostels.

(iii) The victim shall not be compelled to produce the consent of the father of her child for the purpose of the child's admission into any schools or hostels. The State should issue directives to the schools/hostels in this regard.

(iv) The mother's/one parent's name shall be considered enough for admission of the child into any school or hostel.

(v) The name of every qualified woman victim shall be included in the electoral rolls and efforts shall be made to obtain electoral photo identity cards to help the women to exercise their franchise.

Medical Services

(i) The Home shall provide adequate professional physical and psychiatric medical services free of charge to the resident.

(ii) Psychological counselling services shall be provided at lest on a part time basis in health care centers.

(iii) Specialised centers of health shall be set up and maintained to cater to the needs of palliative care for the victims suffering from terminal stages of HIV/AIDs.

(iv) The victims when placed in the shelter home shall be provided with proper medical, psychological care and other necessary professional care including handling of trauma with an assessment of the degree of trauma and a decision on the nature of counselling for the particular victim.

(v) The care staff helping professionals and other functionaries shall be provided with orientation, sensitisation and wherever possible specialised training.

Counselling Services

(i) The Home shall recognise that counselling is a right of the victim and professional counselling services shall be made available that every stage, free of cost for the victims.

(ii) The Home shall appoint on a regular/visiting basis, professionally qualified and experienced counsellors for the assistance of the victims.

(iii) Counseling services should be provided in such a manner that every victim has regular access to a trained counsellor. The nature and frequency of counselling support will depend on factor such as identifiable mental illness, extent of trauma experienced and emotional resilience of the victim. (See also the RVWPP)

(iv) Specialised counselling shall be provided to victims with HIV/AIDS including pre-test, post-test and on going support.

(v) Psycho-social interventions shall be conducted in a private and confidential setting, and shall take into account the recipient's language, culture, age, sex, ethnicity, class and religion.

Legal Assistance

(i) The State/Home shall recognise that legal assistance is a right of the victim and shall ensure that the services of professional legal advisors are made available at very stage free of cost for the victims. (See also the RVWPP)

(ii) The legal assistance shall be provided unconditionally and shall not be conditional to the victim's willingness to serve as witness and thereby cooperate with the Home or the state or the police or any other authority which is concerned with the prosecution of the accused.

(iii) Legal representation for the rescued victim must be wither voluntary and informed consent and in consultation with the support person, if any.

Adherence to the Law

the concerned/relevant magistrate or judicial officer or the members of the competent authority, as the case may be, should visit and supervise the rescue home periodically, preferably once a month, to ensure adherence to court orders and directions.

Prosecution

(i) Effective prosecution is the fulfillment of an important need of the victim of a crime and of the need to belong to a society that is based on principles of fairness and is devoid of arbitrariness. Each home shall make efforts to facilitate prosecution so that the victim can enjoy a sense of justice.

(ii) Care shall be taken to ensure that prosecution does not come in the way of or delay rehabilitation. Every technical administrative measure shall be exhausted to ensure that prosecution is speeded up and the presence and travel by the victims is minimised.

Economic Rehabilitation

(i) Each victim shall be equipped with knowledge, skills, an appropriate attitude and orientation required for her/his economic rehabilitation.

(ii) An Economic Rehabilitation Plan shall be evolved for each victim separately by taking into consideration the victim's individuality and strengths and weaknesses—by a group of experts from different disciplines. (See also Chapter: *Management and Staff*)

(iii) The victim shall have the right to choose her/his Economic Rehabilitation Plan (ERP) and shall be encouraged to participate in its evolution.

(iv) Economic rehabilitation for each victim shall be documented/recorded in the personal file and shall be made accessible to the victim. (See also Chapter: *Management and Staff*)

Vocational Training and Guidance

(i) Vocational training shall be preceded by vocational guidance.

(ii) Vocational guidance shall be planned and carried out professionally.

(iii) Vocational training is an important but only a partial requirement in the process of attaining the goal of economic rehabilitation. The vocational training of victims shall aim at achieving skill levels sufficient for the victims to find either employment in competitive market situations or to start gainful self-employment.

Case Management Systems

(i) State/Homes shall maintain all relevant details on the victims after the rescue process and deal with each victim on a case management basis.

(ii) No rescued victim shall be sent back to the family without adequate assessment and without ensuring social acceptance and family support.

(iii) Every Home shall maintain a victim's confidential and secure record.

(iv) Every victim shall have the right to inquire about such personal records as appropriate.

(v) Each Home shall maintain a health file on each of the resident victims.

(vi) Each Home shall carry out a complete health assessment of the victim within a week after admission.

39. Confidentiality

(i) Complete confidentiality shall be maintained about the facial and other personal identity of the victim. This is valid at all stages from rescue to prosecution and social reintegration and thereafter.

(ii) Every victim shall be helped to fully overcome any sense of guilt, complex, low self image arising out of her special background of commercial sexual exploitation and trafficking. It is advisable to keep the background confidential and not to be revealed without the explicit and informed consent of the victim. Therefore, follow up must be handled with due care not to expose the special background and identity of the victim, as in the absence of a matching change in social perception and a protective environment, such exposures might be used by hostile social elements to her distress.

(iii) Case Management records retained by the Shelter/Home/Center shall be filed in a confidential and protected manner. The privacy and confidentiality of all resident victims and their children (where applicable) as regards their past, residency in the center, or future situation shall be ensured by the shelter/Home/enter. (See also *Case Management*)

Repatriation

(i) No rescued victim shall be sent back to the family without adequate assessment and without ensuring social acceptance and family support. State will ensure that repartriation is carried out depending on how safe and nurturing the family environment is for the victim. If and when the victim chooses to return to an abusive family situation, the State would need to intervene and repatriate the victim to an institution which can protect and care for the individual. Repartriation will be done after the stay in a shelter.

(ii) States shall work out the details of the repatriation procedures and structure and mainstream them in order to facilitate the smooth and efficient repatriation of the victims and their dependent minors.

(iii) The members of the professional and (preferably) voluntary sector organisations who have had some helping interaction with the victim shall be represented in the process of repatriation.

(iv) No rescued victim shall be sent back to the family without fully ensuring that the victim shall not be re-trafficked.

(a) The victim being repatriated should be counselled and prepared to return to the country of origin after providing her with adequate medical and pscho-social care as well as after empowering her through basis life-skills so that she is able to be reintegrated in mainstream life.

(b) State will provide adequate financial assistance for meeting the needs of rescued victims during travel while repatriating them to their families or institutions in source areas.

(c) State will also make adequate provision for dearness

allowance for police escort or any other authorized escort during such travel.

(d) State will also reimburse emergency expenses incurred by the police or other authorised escorts. The State will assign to an appropriate authority the responsibility of adequate follow-up.

(e) Repatriation should be done only with the consent of the victim. While making the decision about repartriation of the rescued victim, the informed consent of a trafficked person shall be sought by the appropriate authority.

Repatriation shall be facilitated by the country of residence by inducting the victim in a structured follow-up programme which ensures: (a) Protection against re-trafficking and against commercial sexual exploitation (b) Protection against Stigma and Discrimination (c) Protection against any other exploitation (d) Optional link with a variety of professional support systems (e) Confidentiality (f) Reorientation (g) Restoration of full citizenship rights (h) Livelihood option (i) Restoration of rights over parental, ancestral and community property and entitlements.

Monthly follow-up should be provided for the first six months and thereafter whenever required, to ensure that the victim receives adequate support and does not get re-trafficked. Adequate follow-up of the victim supervised by the Child Welfare Committee or any other competent authority dealing with women/children along with the close co-operation of other recognised organisations should be mandatory for a period of three years after the victim has been repartriated.

Movement in and out of Shelter

All efforts should be made to persuade and motivate victim of trafficking and other forms of violence to be reintegrated and rehabilitated in society to lead a dignified life.

State shall ensure that no rescued victims is sent back to the family without ensuring social acceptance and family support to the victim in order to prevent re-trafficking and further commercial sexual exploitation.

State, in collaboration with appropriate government or non-governmental organisations should provide entrepreneurship development training which will include skills, knowledge, and resources, marketing skills and micro-credit at district level.

Each victim who leaves the Home including those who complete the process of economic rehabilitation shall be equipped with knowledge, instruments, and mechanisms, confidence, art and skills of reverting to the Home or any other source of professional care and support when in need of the same.

Upon discharge, each victim shall be provided with her educational records, medical records, legal documents, and other means such as savings and personal belongings.

The Home shall conduct outreach/support activities, or shall oversee the delegation of those activities to other organisations or individuals in accordance with the Reintegration Plan. Outreach/ support activities shall be conducted only with the consent of the victims.

Outreach/support activities shall include counseling support visits to assist in counseling upon reintegration to the victims/ family/relatives and local community people.

In trafficking cases where the entry of the victim in he Rescue Home is very late (e.g. the Home is meant for residents/ victims up to the age of 18 and the victim enters at the age of 17) there is a need to extend the protective cover of residential services for a longer period. Some protective cover for the rescued person shall continue even after reintegration through Drop-in Centres, and After-Care Homes.

Linking with Support Systems

Every victim shall be gradually, systematically and professionally linked to a variety of support system and given the skill and confidence to avail herself of these systems. Considering the fact that ups and downs are inevitable in any person's life, provision shall be made to offer support services for use by the victim even after a certain degree of rehabilitation and social reintegration. These services shall not create any obstacle in the reintegration process by revealing the identity of the victim. This will be achieved by setting up Drop-in Centers and follow-up activities as well as by building up confidence among the victims to make use of those support services when required.Positive intervention of the state may end with social reintegration. Thereafter, the trafficked and rehabilitated person should be able, in case of need, to fall back on a support system established jointly by the government and voluntary sector organisations for that purpose.

Management/Resources

The Homes shall introduce professionalism in their management practices.

Regardless of the selection and appointment of trained staff the Home shall have its staff, particularly those who are directly engaged in service delivery and thus come in contact with the victims, re-trained periodically.

Every member of the staff shall be oriented to the problem of commercial sexual exploitation and trafficking and the psycho-social situation of the victims as well as the protocols, conventions, legal provisions, rules and regulations at the time of posting. The staff so oriented shall be administered a brief test in order to ensure that she/he has understood the special requirements and Do's and Don'ts of working in the Home with the victims.

Complaints Procedure

The Home shall evolve and mainstream a rational procedure of registering victims' complaints about the managerial and other aspects of the Home. The registered complaints shall be periodically made available to the external monitoring/steering committee. The Home shall ensure that the right of the victims to complain to the highest authority shall be carefully guarded. Each Home shall evolve and maintain a confidential complaints procedure.

Each Home shall notify legal authorities and legal guardians in cases of accidents, deaths, or runaways. Each Home shall introduce and protect mechanisms for prompt and sure reporting of incidences of bullying, physical and sexual exploitation or harassment, injury, physical or verbal abuse, of the victim.

Home staff shall be trained to deal with and share information which they are given in confidence for victim protection purposes. Every complain shall be addressed without delay and the complaint is to be kept informed of the progress of action taken by the authority on her complaint.

State shall periodically remind the Home authorities about the legal and other accountability of the Homes towards the victims.

Monitoring

Every care and support activity run by the State shall be monitored closely and reviewed periodically. The concerned/relevant magistrate or judicial officer or the members of the competent authority, as the case may be, should visit and supervise the rescue home, periodically, preferably once a month to ensure adherence to court orders and directions. (See also the RVWPP)

Internet/cyberspace based systems of sharing important information on the victim (with due care for confidentiality) among the various social agencies shall be mainstreamed to maximise the utilisation of resources and efforts, minimise wastage and reduce the chances of relapse or re trafficking.

Each member of the staff should be familiar with the Standards of service and behaviour which they are required to meet. This should be a working document readily available and accessed by all staff.

These quality standards shall be used while undertaking supervision and performance appraisal or for assessing staff performance. The standards should be regularly discussed at staff meetings and a shared assessment be made about the extent to which good practices are being achieved and areas for development of the service. Standards should be regularly reviewed at a senior management level in the organisation in order to assess the strengths of services provided to victims, any resource gaps and areas for training and professional development.

Communication and action at all levels regarding the monitoring and review of standards of victims' care should serve to ensure that adherence to the relevant United Nations conventions/ instruments is a demonstrable reality for all victims.

The staff of the Home shall be adequately gender sensitized prior to being posted in the Home and shall undergo periodical in-service training for gender sensitivity

The victims shall be trained and retrained in First Aid. The Home shall have its staff trained in First Aid. The trained staff shall be re-trained periodically to ensure proper and efficient application of First Aid.

The Home shall ensure that the victims are encouraged to meet staff, regularly, individually or in groups, to discuss the general running of the home, to plan activities and to make their views known. The Home shall try to avoid marking the transport vehicle used by the Home for the movement of the victims in any such way as to distinguish it from a normal car or bus. Care shall be taken not to reveal the identity of the category of the victims. A senior and high level official of the Home shall personally approve the Economic Rehabilitation Plan (ERP) and periodically assess process for each victim.

ANNEXURE

National Policy on Women (Preliminary Draft)

The principles of gender equality and gender justice have been basic to Indian thinking and have been enshrined in the Indian Constitution in its Preamble, Fundamental Rights and Directive Principles. Article 14 guarantees justice—social, economic and political—as well as equality before law and ensures non-discrimination on the basis of sex. Article 15(3) empowers the State to make special provisions for the promotion of the welfare and development of women.

India has committed herself to equal rights and inherent human dignity of women and men by ratifying various international human rights instruments, particularly the convention on the elimination of all Forms of Discrimination Against Women. India is form in its resolve of full implementation of the human rights of women and the girl child as an inalienable, integral and indivisible part of all human rights and fundamental freedoms. The Mexico Plan of Action, the Nairobi forward Looking strategies and the Beijing declaration as well as the Platform for Action have been unreservedly endorsed.

Acknowledging that the empowerment of women can best be achieved through their full participation in the political process, the 73rd and 74th Constitutional Amendment Acts have provided reservation of one third of all seats and posts of chairpersons for women in institutions of local governance, both rural and urban.

The Report of the Committee on the Status of Women in India, the National Perspective Plant for Women and the Shramshakti report highlighted the prevalent discrimination against women and Recommended various measures for the advancement of women. Many of these recommendations are reflected in the plans and action programmes as well as amendments to various laws in the country.

A 'strong women' movement representing a vibrant force and a well spread out network of non-governmental organisations, with their intellectual strength, grassroots presence and committed approach to women's issues have been successfully inspiring many of these policies and helping to carry them out effectively.

The Constitutional commitment has been reflected in our development plans and policies. These have recognised women as equal partners and have aimed for their economic, social and political empowerment. The plans are determined to ensure that the benefits of development from different sectors do not bypass women.

A number of States have also come out with policies and Action Plans for Women. The Central/State Social Welfare Boards, State Departments of Women's Development and Women's Development Corporations, National Commission for Women and several State Commissions for Women have been set up to improve the status of women and to safeguard their legal rights. A number of schemes and programmes have been initiated, particularly with a view to their economic advancement and social deference.

The experience since Independence has made us realise, however, the stark reality that these exists a wide gap between the goals of our constitution and the de facto situation of women in India. That they lag behind in all spheres of life is very clear. The balance of gender equality, justice and equity continues to be titled towards men. Thee are many obstacles for women to overcome. Women in India continue to bear the burden of poverty, illiteracy, economic marginalisation, exclusion from decision making, lack of access to resources, social stereotyping, discrimination an violence at household and societal levels. There is a persistent and institutionalised discrimination against the girl-child and mechanisms to achieve gender equality, justice and equity remain inadequate to meet the situation.

In order to effect the advancement and empowerment of women and bring about a marked improvement in their status before the next millennium, it is imperative to strongly India's unflinching commitment to the cause, hopes, aspirations and visions of Indian women through a comprehensive Policy. This will focus on institutional and structural factors that have continued to perpetuate the low status of and discrimination against women.

The Policy shall be integrated into all macro-level initiatives which shall henceforth be taken by the State. It shall, on a regular and on-going basis, guide and inform action at all levels. It shall thus give a very clear mandate to all institutions of governance, public and private, to mainstream women's issues, their advancement and empowerment.

A. Policy

The following goals shall be achieved through the Policy:

1. Creation of an environment which promotes de facto equality between women and men.
2. Mainstreaming women's perspectives and women's issues in all polities, plans and programmes in public and private spheres.
3. Support to women's movement and NGOs in achieving women' rights and equality.
4. Facilitation of affirmative action for women's equal participation at all levels of decision making.
5. Enhancement and utilization of the human capital potential of women.
6. Elimination of all form of discrimination against women, girl children and adolescent girls.
7. Increase in the involvement of women and men in devel-

opment processes and the creation of a just social order.

8. Equal opportunities for men and women, through out their lives, in every sphere.

B. The Policy shall therefore ensure the following

1. That women and men enjoy, in practice, equal rights, equal access to and control over productive resources, education, health, land, other forms of property, shelter, credit, information, knowledge, skills, technology, markets, etc. by adopting positive and affirmative action, wherever necessary and removing identified impediments.

(a) Equal access to full employment, literacy, nutrition and all aspects of health-care.

2. That women and men benefit equally from all development efforts.

3. The laws policies, rules and regulations do not discriminate against women in any way including in their outcomes and that they affirm full participation and equality for women.

4. That all new policies, plans and programmes are drawn up with the full and equal participation of women and with women's perspectives.

5. That women's contribution to the national economy is acknowledged, valued, reflected and disseminated.

(a) That data be collected on all issues relating to women.

6. That collection of all statistics by Central/State Statistical Organisations, Bureaus, Departments/Ministries and other institutions in the public and the private sector is on a gender disaggregated basis.

7. That women's groups and collectives at the grassroots level are promoted and strengthened.

8. That the importance of support services for the empowerment and advancement of women is recognised and

appropriately reflected in sectoral policies and programme.

9. That the needs of special groups of women such as disabled and elderly women, women-headed households, women of the unorganised and informal sector, internally displaced women, as well as inter-State migrant women workers are given special attention in sectoral policies and programmes.

10. That there is a convergence of welfare, development and related support services for women to ensure improved access and greater impact.

11. That there is full and equal participation of women in all for a and levels and processes of decision making, in all sectors, including legislative, executive, and judicial institutions, in order to achieve parity in representation of women and men therein.

12. Elimination of all forms of violence and atrocities against women, girl-children, and adolescent girls in public and private spheres. Public servants responsible for administration of law and order shall be made specifically accountable for enforcing laws relating to such atrocitics.

13. That the positive portrayal of women is promoted and all stereo-typed and degrading images of women in all forms of media public and private, are eliminated.

14. That the realisation of the full potential of girl-children, adolescent girl and women is facilitated and that a sense of their self-esteem and self worth is developed through all sectoral programmes, public and private.

15. That sensitisation of all persons be attempted through awareness generation programmes on the equality between women and men for the transformation of the social mindset.

16. That men and women of all sections of society, including non-governmental organisations, cooperative sector, trade unions, political parties, corporate sector, educational institutions, etc. are involved in the development, advance-

ment and empowerment process of women.

17. That research and technology development aim to remove drudgery from the lives of girl-children and women.

C. The Policy prescribes, inter-alia, the following specific strategies for action

1. The existing machinery for women's advancement, development and empowerment at the National and State levels shall be suitably strengthened and appropriate structures created at Parliament/State Legislatures to review that all policies and programmes contribute to improvement of the status of women.

2. All Central and State Ministries shall draw up time bound Action Plans for translating the Policy into a set of concrete actions, within six months of the announcement of the Policy.

3. There shall be at the Central and State Levels a National/State Committee which shall in tandem with Central/State ministries/Departments of women's development, the National/State Social Welfare Boards, National/State Commissions for Women, different Ministries/Departments, and non-Governmental Organisations, oversee the implementation of the policy. The Annual Report of the Committee shall be tabled in the Parliament/State Legislature.

4. Every State Government shall prepare a State Profile on Women.

5. A Gender Development Index for Women shall be prepared by Central and State Governments to facilitate planning, implementation, review and evaluation of policies, and programmes.

6. Every Ministry/Department of the Centre/State shall make provisions for equal participation of women in their programmes/activities. They shall also identify actual benefits, both in physical and financial terms accruing to women through its different Plans and Programmes ex-

ecuted directly or through autonomous organsations and public undertakings working under it and shall report annually to parliament/State Legislature in this regard.

7. Planning Commission may ensure that the Central and State Governments identify separately specific resources allocated for women and men particularly in the sectors of education, training and skill development.

(a) The National Development Council shall review all development programmes and targets on the basis of gender disaggregated data and ensure, with the support of the Planning commission, flow of funds for programmes undertaken for women in various sectors.

(b) In the sectors of education, training and skill development, income generation and health, the allocation of resources shall be identified separately for women and men.

8. Gender sensitisation programmes for personnel in all institutions, public and private at all levels shall be organised on a regular basis. These shall include the executive, legislative and judicial wings of the State.

9. All sectoral policies, already in place, shall be suitably amended to reflect the National Policy on Women.

10. All Commissions, committees and other decision making bodies in the public and private sector shall aim to give equal representation to women.

11. The private sector shall aim at integrating the principles of the Policy in their programmes and functioning.

Bibliography

Agarwal, R.S., and Sarvesh Kumr (1986), *Crimes and Punishment in New Perspective*, Mittal Publications, New Delhi.

Ahuja Ram, *Social problems in India*, Rawat Publications, New Delhi,1993.

Bandura, A. (1973), Aggression: A SocialLEARNIGN Analysis, Englewood Cliffs: Prentice Hall.

Benson, Donna (1977), Sexual Harassment: A Hidden Issue, Published by Projection the Status of Womne, Association of American College.

Brodsky, Annette. M (1975, (ed)., The Female Offender, London: sage Publications.

Burra Neera, *Born to Work: Child Labour in India*, Oxford University Press, New Delhi 1995

Bureau of Police Research and Development (1983), *Crime in India 1979*, New Delhi: Bureau of Research and Development, Ministry of Home Affairs, Government of India.

Cloward, Richard A. and LLOYD E. Ohlin (1960), Delinquency and Opportunity: A Theory of Delinquent Gangs, Glencoe, III.: Foree Press.

Cohen, Albert K., (1955), Delinquent Boys: tehCulture of the Gang, Glencoe, III: Free Press.

Diwan, Paras (1983), *Family Law: Law of Marriage and in India*, New Delhi: Sterling Publishers.

Everett, J.M. (1979), Women and Social change in India. New Delhi, Heritage Publishers.

Farley, Lin (1978), Sexual Shaedown, New Yorik: McGraw Hill.

Fox, G.L. (1977), "Female Delinquency," in O. Wilson (ed.), Delinquency inAustralia: A critical Appraisal, queensland: University Press.

Gelles, R.J. (1972), tehViolent Home, beverly Hills: Sage Publicastions.

Goode, W.J, (1974), "Force and Violence in th efamily," in Steinmet and Strauss (ed.), Violence in the Family, New York: Harpess and Row.

Government of India (1988), Natonal perspective Plan for Women 1988-2000 A.D., Deptt. of Women and Child Development, Ministry of Human Resoruce Development.

Hilberman, E. and Munson, M. 91978), "Sixty Battered Women," *Victimology, An International Journal*, 1977-78, pp. 460-471. quoted by woldfgang and Weiner "Criminal Violence.

Jayal, Shakambari (1966), *The Status of Women in the Epics*, Delhi, Motilal Banarasidass.

Kapadia, K.W. (1966), *Marriage and Family in India*, London, Oxford University Press.

Krishnamurthy, S. (1981), *The Dowry Problem: A Legal and Social Perspective*, Bangalore, IBH Prakashan.

Mamoria, C.B. (1981), *Social Problems and Social Disorganisation in India*, Kitab Mahal, Allahabad.

Nair, P.T. (1979), *Marriage and Dowry in India*. Calcutta.

Panikkar, .M. (1961), *Hindu Society at Cross Roads*, London.

Paul, M.C. (1986), Dowry and Position of WomeninIndia, Delhi.

Quinney, Richard (1977), teh social Reality of crime, Boston,

Rai Usha, *Life in the Right Track Parenting*, January, 1997.

Ray, Dunu, *Rights of Child Labour*, Ethics: Production and Nationwide Economic & Political weekly, January 31, 1998.

Remington Franceise, Child Labour: Without a Global Response. *Economic and Political Weekly*, December 28, 1996.

Shogan, W.G., and M.G. Maxfield 91981), *Coping with Crime Victimisation*, Fer, and Reactions to Crime in three American Cities, Beverly Hills: C.A. Sage.

Shogan, W.G., and M.g. Maxfield (1981), *Coping with Crime: Victimisation*. Fear, and Reactions to Crime in three American Cities, Bevrly Hills: C.A. Sage.

thomas, P. (1961, *Women and Marriage in India*. London..

Trinklenberg, J.R. (1973), "Alcohol and Violence," In bourne and Fox (eds.), Alcoholism Progress in Research and Treatment, New York: Academic Press.

Walker, L.F. (1977-78), "Battered Women and Learned Helplessness," *Victimology*.